ONE EYE OPEN

MELISSA M. SACHS

ONE EYE OPEN

MELISSA M. SACHS

One Eye Open
Copyright © 2017 by Melissa Holmes-Sachs

All rights reserved. No portion of this publication may be reproduced, stored in a retrieval system, or transmitted by any means—electronic, mechanical, photocopying, recording, or any other—except for brief quotations in printed reviews, without the prior written permission of the publisher.

This book is not a substitute for ongoing professional management by your health care provider if required. Neither the publisher nor the author is responsible for any damage, medical or otherwise, resulting from following the suggestions in this book.

Editors: Earl Tillinghast, Hamishe Randall, Regina Cornell

Cover Design: Lucas Art & Design
Interior Design: Whitney Evans, SGR-P Formatting Services

Indigo River Publishing
3 West Garden Street Ste. 352
Pensacola, FL 32502
www.indigoriverpublishing.com

Ordering Information:

Quantity sales: Special discounts are available on quantity purchases by corporations, associations, and others. For details, contact the publisher at the address above.

Orders by U.S. trade bookstores and wholesalers: Please contact the publisher at the address above.

Printed in the United States of America

Library of Congress Control Number: 2017954787
ISBN: 978-0-9990210-6-4

First Edition

With Indigo River Publishing, you can always expect great books, strong voices, and meaningful messages. Most importantly, you'll always find...words worth reading.

CONTENTS

Thank You and Dedication — vii
Preface — xi
Introduction — xv

1. Big Mistakes and Bigger Regrets — 1
2. Terrified of the Man I Love and Hate: Husband Number Two — 7
3. A Dream Gone and I Am Still Here, or Am I? — 11
4. How I Got Here — 15
5. Open Your Eyes, Stupid — 23
6. A Slow Death but Still Trying to Make it Work — 33
7. Instead of Leaving I Get Married: Living the Trauma Bond and Co-dependency — 39
8. Time Warp — 45
9. The Lion and His Lion Blanket — 47
10. What Trust? — 51
11. Coma — 53
12. Not My Normal — 55
13. Time Warp Two — 59
14. Yet Another Failed Attempt to Leave — 63
15. Planning to Elope — 69
16. Vegas — 73
17. Eighteen Days Later — 75
18. This isn't Love — 79
19. Pain — 81
20. The Party — 85
    Conclusion — 91
    ADDENDUM: Finding like survivors saved my life — 93
    WHAT TO LOOK FOR TO AVOID A NARCISSISTIC, ABUSIVE RELATIONSHIP: — 95
    APPENDIX — 113

THANK YOU AND DEDICATION

I want to thank the people in my family who couldn't understand but tried to stand by me anyway. I won't name names, but thanks to the dog sitters and to the ones who let me stay at their homes during my failed attempts to leave, tolerating last-minute hysterical show ups—sometimes with the police and always with a dog or two. I want to thank my friends who let me weep and complain, who listened without judgement. I also want to thank the people in my family who exited my life because they couldn't stand to see me stay; I miss you and I forgive you. I hope, someday, you know anything I said or did was out of needing you in my life and that I still want that.

I especially want to thank my children for trusting me, even though I made a mistake. I hope someday you understand and make better choices throughout your lives. The lost time with you is something I will never forgive myself for. Focusing on something, someone, so broken that he almost broke me, too, is something that made me less of a parent during those years; and for that, I am deeply sorry.

A special thank you to my publisher, Indigo River, for giving me this opportunity and especially to one of my editors, Earl Tillinghast, for your endless patience and expertise. I hope we get to work together again!

This book is dedicated to all those who didn't make it through the tunnel. To their parents, friends, and loved ones: they were never WEAK; they were abused and couldn't handle the pain. My hope is that this story is used as a resource to help anyone in an abusive relationship. May God give you the strength to leave.

A SEMICOLON IS USED WHEN AN AUTHOR COULD'VE CHOSEN TO END THEIR SENTENCE, BUT CHOSE NOT TO; THE AUTHOR IS YOU AND THE SENTENCE IS YOUR LIFE.

Project Semicolon

A movement dedicated for people who struggle with self-harm, addiction, and suicide; many resulting from abuse.

PREFACE

There have been many stories written about domestic abuse, but what makes mine different is that I wrote this while I was still actually with the monster. Without having any labels for what was happening to me at that time, it is raw, real and true. My fight to find love nearly killed me.

Most of these other stories seem to send the message that if I warn one person, or stop one person from meeting one of these devils, then it was worth it. I disagree because I don't believe it works that way. I wish it did. I never listened; I never looked for signs and have since learned I was not unique. This story is for **survivors,** the ones in it now, the ones trying to leave, and the ones broken on the floor, trying to understand. I needed to understand *while* it was happening, while I was making attempts to leave, and while I was in the middle of an almost ten-year abusive relationship, in which I was terrorized and threatened; mentally, physically and sexually abused; lied to; cheated on; and simultaneously told how loved I was. I had never heard the words "trauma bond" or "love bombing," and I was depressed and alone—my whole family had turned on me, blaming me for staying, but how could they know if I didn't?

PREFACE

I didn't know! It took years for me to know. His money and power demanded respect. It took me almost five years to get out of my own head, my own pain, to finally see, to actually *believe* what I was seeing, to accept what I knew to be true, and even more time after that to leave for good. I left six times and married him before I was able to end it. I was addicted to figuring it out, to finding out why, and to the pain. I hoped he would change, that I might understand him and believe his words. Finally, I realized that it would never happen; he didn't care, and he never would. I was nothing to him and could be instantly replaced. The narcissistic sociopath inside of him was real. He terrified me. Not only did he abuse me but he destroyed my irreplaceable property when I tried to leave, including baby videos and my car. Despite all of this and the fact he tried to kill me by running me off the road more than once, what was even worse was the realization that I still loved him (or thought I did).

I tried to help him, told myself I didn't want a second divorce, told myself that he loved me back, found him doctors, diagnoses (was he bi-polar, autistic?), outlets for his rage and anger—all to no avail. I researched his "symptoms;" I catered to his every need and looked for any excuse for his brutal behavior. He actually got madder the calmer and more supportive I became. It was then I realized that only if I left for good would I be free of him. We could never discuss or resolve any issues, and he always pulled me back in before I knew what hit me, but I was getting smarter. I learned later that their only fuel is to drink the goodness from those around them. They drain any goodness, loyalty, and, most of all, any **emotion**, especially anger and pain. They don't want to change, do you hear me? They don't *want* to.

I wrote this for you so you can hear sooner, so you can see. I want you to run. Some of you may not make it if you don't realize that they are the ones with the problem, that playing you is their favorite pastime. Some of you have tried and not made it yet. I almost didn't. I didn't want to end my life; I just wanted the pain to stop, to try again, and to get out. Just as it was for me, your life is on the other side of this nightmare.

We have to look hard at why they target us at all and why we allow it. We are not victims; we are enlightened survivors. Once you realize that point, once you drag yourself through the tunnel of hell and admit you have to heal and feel the loss of loving a monster, you can then feel the awesome power of looking in the mirror and see yourself grow and change. You need to see your own patterns and co-dependence and how this may have led you to choose everything except yourself. This is a time that you can actually change your life and actually be grateful for that.

For me, it was one serious relationship to the next, starting at the age of sixteen for almost thirty years, that finally ended up in an almost-decade-long abusive relationship and losing everything. But losing everything meant waking up and finally gaining myself and my freedom.

Being alone, with nothing, and finally starting my life and actually LIVING it—or dying in a pool of depression, those were my choices—I chose to dig deep and live. I chose to change.

INTRODUCTION

Family history and your childhood: does it matter?

I always thought I was strong, but after this last experience, I really have to look back, look at myself and what made me behave in certain ways, so I can avoid making the same mistakes. So yes, it matters—a lot. My parents were very young when they got married; my mom, pregnant at 16. There was a lot of fighting, infidelity, and unhappiness. My mother, who raised me, was unhappy my entire childhood. I spent a lot of time alone and truly missed having my father in my life on a regular basis. I did not fulfill myself or my dreams. I was in a very emotionally-dependent relationship at the age of 16. I got married at 25 and was in a very emotionally-dependent marriage. He was a good man, but I was not whole. A healthy relationship should add to who you are, not *be who you are*. I believed all I needed was love and stability, but what I really needed was to fulfill my own passions and goals first, to have pride and purpose. That is why I was such a good target for a narcissist, because I still believed the **right** love would make me happy, fill my voids. Some of us go into relationships, not realizing it, to fill the spaces, and that is always a mistake. We

INTRODUCTION

have to be happy, whole, and healthy to be in relationships or they won't work.

    I now have to look hard at what I was numbing, what I was putting in the place of me, what I did wrong and can do better now. I have to see my own weaknesses, patterns and mistakes, to learn without blame, to be stronger. I can tell you without a doubt, the selfless love of my first husband nearly had me loving myself. After my marriage ended I felt broken and guilty because my children were now victims of divorce. This feeling of brokenness led me away from dealing with my own issues to become a better, stronger, more independent person. Only now, after being beaten and left for emotionally dead, have I, ironically, the strength to stand on my own two feet. My wish for you? See to your dreams! Set your goals in life, get your education, and be proud of what you do, contribute to the community, create the life that you love, and sustain yourself. Be **healthy** and recognize what you have to offer, standards and morals of love, loyalty, joy, sacrifice, self-care. But most of all, listen to your instincts. If something feels off it most likely is. If someone's treatment of you feels *less* than what you know you deserve, or what you have to offer them, it is. These monsters cannot be saved. Please don't try. Learn what a healthy, loving, give-and-take relationship is, offer it and demand it in return. Learn what a toxic, unhealthy, one-sided relationship is, and avoid it or end it immediately, at all costs, because the cost is way too high, trust me. And one more thing, if a friend or loved one tells you they need help, and you don't really understand their behavior because it looks like they are choosing to be abused, please help them. You can get them books or phone numbers and lend an ear. Help them see, to find the local women's resource center and domestic abuse hotlines—you could save a life.

1

BIG MISTAKES AND BIGGER REGRETS

A fool, I am a fool. I don't know how I got here or why I am even here again. Home? I feel the tightness tighten inside of me, its grip never really loosening. I need to focus, to think, to plan, to get away from him once and for all. *Stick to it*, I tell myself but everything hurts. I feel judged, hopeless, angry at being put in this positon. I make choices—to leave, choose life, happiness, forgive myself, move on—then the immediate crash, his kind, harassing words pulling me back. His promises take me away from their judging eyes. My family, my neighbors, my friends, my co-workers all think that I am normal, but I am not. I need a rope to get me up this hill and out of this mess. But they don't see it, and they don't see him throw the rope and me grab on to it either, as I totally forget he is the one who put me here. I also forget how much it burns and scrapes, as blood runs down my legs and I climb back to him. No one can see me now, no one is helping me —but no one knows he is a monster.

I left the perfect life for this. Divorced after fifteen years and craving the love I thought I needed, finding the relationship I always thought I wanted… The alpha male I am with now is a malignant, narcissistic sociopath. I had never even known what those words meant. He is so dangerous, and I am losing myself in the never-ending cycle of pain. He will let me go—he has to. I will wait, make him hate me, get bored, save money. I pray it will happen soon—time is running out…my soul is dying.

Why is this happening to me? Why do I have to live this, to learn it? Maybe to save one of my children from it one day, maybe to save you.

* * *

So now, I have to tell my story from the end and then go back to the beginning. It was never him I loved, just the dream of what I wanted. And even though I had no idea such evil existed, and even though I now know it has a name, I am still in pain, still mad, still having to pick up the pieces of my life, of my soul. At least now I know I am not crazy, as he says. At least now I know he cannot ever love me back, or anyone for that matter. Knowing does help; it distracts me from feeling entirely alone. I have those who have given it a name, those who have suffered like me. Like I am now. It diminishes the depression enough to see the light, enough to let go of the rage one drop at a time, enough to stop blaming myself.

But first—ouch!, OMG, ouch!—I have to get through the next ten minutes while the nice man finishes using the needle on me, putting permanent ink into my wrist forever. I like it and I hate it; the pain helps me focus on remembering to never let him back in, to never listen to his words or his lies ever again. The tattoo will remind me that I want a divorce; I am the one who wants it, even though I feel like a part of me is dead, rejected, failing. It will remind me why I suggested a mediator and not a fight with someone who can't lose because he has no conscience or feelings or regret. It reminds me that, even if I struggle and I have to eat cereal for dinner, I have this. It says, "FREEDOM" and I love it. Freedom, in my case, is being hard earned. I wish I could thank him; I wish I could say I learned something amazing and valuable, but at this point, I really can't—the pain is too potent.

He ruined everything. I am done, and I wanted to share everything with him. I learned that what I was experiencing had a name, and even though it took me a few years to figure it out, it has all happened before. I try to think of a reason I had to learn it all, to feel it all, to almost die from it.

* * *

HE FORGOT MY BIRTHDAY. I am moving into my own house with my daughter in a month, so I still live here, and he forgot my birthday. I didn't want him to remember, and I hoped he didn't remember, and I never want to share anything with him ever again. But he forgot my birthday, and it still makes me feel rejected, unimportant, less. I have tools now, though, and I have websites like Psychopathfree.com to reference, where my pain and thoughts and "recovery" are mirrored, and this helps. It helps me not to tell him he forgot or to show emotions to him or to let the rejection take anymore pieces of me away. It helps me not to tell my sister, who will never understand, why it hurts he forgot my birthday, why the rejection messes with my being, why the pain is the greatest thing I have ever felt, and why it has threatened my entire sanity, my future, my life. It helps. Then the day is over and I am okay.

So now, we can go back to where it began, to where I thought I was in love, to a place when I was innocent, a believer, ignorant of true evil. I left a 15-year marriage to a great guy, a great dad, but he was an addict—maybe not illegal drugs, but alcohol was enough to make me leave, enough to make me tell myself, *This is not the life I want.* I was wrong, but that is ancient history now. My ex is kind, selfless, loving, soft-spoken, honest, affectionate. I often feel like I am being mean to him just by being me. Jay, my second husband, is mean, sick, demanding. "No" is never an option for him. He demands what he wants, and he always gets it. Not this time. I used to want some of that: being so sure, never taking no for an answer. He is very obsessed and busy at work, always **telling** everyone **how** to do **everything**. No one can ever do anything right; no one ever lives up to his expectations or does it as good as he can, according to him. When he does come "home," which is whenever he wants, he eats, watches sleazy television and falls asleep, the volume always too high.

Yes, my (first) ex-husband gives and gives. He gives great massages, gets me my favorite iced tea…He is a hands-on dad and works a full-time job and coaches three sports a year at a high school. It was not only the drinking that impacted our relationship. He wanted something from me that I could not give him. He wanted everything to always be the same, for our lives to never change, including the lamps staying on the same tables in the living room. He wants what we have to be enough. He grew up with an amazing family. He had sameness—same house, same friends, same job—his whole life. I have never experienced this. I moved from Queens, New York, to Nassau, Bahamas, as a child because of my father's hotel job; and when my parents got divorced, he literally left us in New Jersey at his sister's house. I moved five more times before high school. I do not know sameness. It is one of the things, looking back, that attracted me to him, husband number one. I could be better because of him, I could have kids that were not like me, that had roots. The American dream, right? Honestly, it is. The thing is, I couldn't change, not even for them. I am a free spirit; I am funny, loyal, loving, ever changing and growing and very adaptable. Whoever made me feel like I was less (mean voice in my head), I am not.

What is it like to be married to an alcoholic? Well, my husband would go outside and lay down in the driveway with my kids. They would look at the stars together and were present and vibrant. He taught then to swim and ride bikes, and we would read to them every night. He never yelled or was impatient. He was attentive and a hard worker. He was affectionate and kind. But that was only him sober. I had a drink once in fifteen years because, with three kids, I felt one of us had to be aware all the time.

What I liked most about him, husband number one, was our ability to communicate. We just talked, and it was great. I loved walking the dog with him and laughing, too. But every time we would go out to dinner, I would leave with a different person than I entered the restaurant with. He was in control on the way in and sleepy and dopey on the way out. If I went downstairs for a glass of water at night, the man I saw a few hours earlier had changed. He was slurring and walking into walls. He was never rude or loud—he was just drunk. The next day I would say, "I didn't even know we had any alcohol in the house," and find his hidden cooler in the garage. I wanted to help him, but he didn't think he had a problem. I went to meetings to find answers, but they talked about everything but the problem. I didn't want friends; I wanted my husband to stop drinking. But I realized later that he had to want that, not me. I asked him once if he was unhappy, and he told me he was the happiest man alive. I left and broke all of our hearts because I couldn't live that way anymore

We had a sad, amicable, attorneyless divorce. He has full access to our children and joint custody at my suggestion. He offered me lifetime alimony, which I took. I stayed home (even though I had a haircutting business for ten years, went to community college, and taught fitness classes), and he worked a lot more hours, obtained his second masters while we were together and made a ton more money than me.

It is so (not) funny how I now want *exactly* what we had together. I have to get it for myself now, now that I am so damaged and torn and broken. I have to get it for myself so no one can ever take it away. I live for the day I can shut the door at the end of the day and have peace, to decide if I want to say "yes" or "no" and to turn off my damn phone. I miss me! I used to be so happy. I have glimpses now and then of the old me, the real me, the unafraid me. I have to, finally, make all of the choices I have allowed men to choose for me my whole life. I have trusted them, put my dreams into them, but those feelings belong to me. I can't share anymore—I won't. I won't be hurt anymore, lose anymore. I am finally enough.

2

TERRIFIED OF THE MAN I LOVE AND HATE: HUSBAND NUMBER TWO

I haven't slept in years. I walk around all day trying to wake up. I wake up tired and power through. I take 20-minute naps in the middle of the day, where I lay there and my heart just races. All…because…of…him. The man I willingly gave up everything for, the man I give my whole heart to, without ever thinking of the risk, of myself. I never had a chance. I put all of my chances into him. The monster.

Remember: when I left my first marriage, I had lifetime alimony; we used a mediator, never fought, and I moved an hour away to start my life. I opened a spin studio and bought a beautiful house I could afford. I moved in that August and met Jay soon after, online, that October. Regret would be an understatement.

I had a wonderful life, both in New Jersey and my new small-town home in northeastern Pennsylvania. I had friends, family nearby, goals, and loved the new school my kids attended. I left an amazing life to create a new amazing life. I left a place I fit in, I belonged, and created a self-induced ripple effect to make the changes I decided I wanted, to be a better mother, a happier, more authentic me. And it all back-fired.

I was played by the master player, and I am too tired to be mad anymore. I am less scared now, too. I have gotten too good at placating him so he sleeps. Old, though…yes, I am very old now at 47. I guess I still look good for my age: 5-feet, 9-inches, 145 pounds, long hair, green eyes. It is my eyes that appear dead to me now, dead tired.

* * *

IT HAS BEEN over a month since he touched me, and while I hate him and wish him dead, I do have needs. I am walking around Wegmans Supermarket, thinking to myself, *Hey, you really do look good today. Why doesn't he love you?* Catching myself with these thoughts is like pulling me off the edge but also like facing the sickness. The sickness is being addicted or bonded to a man who treats you like the dirt on his shoe, being addicted to the "whys." Why doesn't he love me back? Why does he say he loves me and cheat on me? Why does he become verbally abusive and physically abusive and I end up accepting his apology? You have no idea what is happening or how to heal until you have the strength to go "no contact" with these demons. It is a roller coaster with no exit.

He was in a rare calm mood last night, and he laid there totally still in a TV trance on the bed while I folded the laundry. He occasionally grabbed my arm, as if he needed me to lay down with him, never taking his eyes off the TV. He is 6-feet, 2-inches tall and muscular; has light brown hair he wears short, as it is thinning; his face is strong and handsome; his eyes, green like mine; his voice, deep. His eyes are sly and sneaky, though, and he never laughs or smiles—years later I wonder how I could possibly have never noticed this. Humor is **everything** in life. After seven years of being together, I really didn't know much about him, and I came to the stunning realization that it is because there isn't anything there. Literally nothing—no substance, no standards, no morals. He has a greed for money and an ego bigger than Texas.

I tell him to stop grabbing me, as the static cling from my daughter's shirt shoots sparks at me. "Just lay down for a minute," he demands softly; but I know it is a type of order because he won't stop until he gets whatever he wants, whenever he wants. I used to think this was a good quality, sexy even. Now I am just his prisoner, and I do his bidding to keep the peace. He suddenly loses patience and grabs me and swings me over his legs, hitting my butt on the way down. He lightly wraps one arm across my stomach, his fingers accidentally grazing my hip. I tell myself this is warmth, and I crave it. I hear his heartless heart inside his big, mean chest; and for a second, I feel loved, wanted. But I know it is a lie, so I don't.

Eventually, he pulls down my pants and takes what he wants. There is no kiss, no caress. There is no tease, no anticipation, no eye contact. He never even looks at me, and although I find this most bizarre, insane, and sad, I still want him to look at me, feel something, not act like this is okay or normal—because if it is then **I am** crazy. But I am not; this is just all a lie. I know him. I have seen the monster inside, always ready, never really dormant. I sleep with one eye open so I don't forget, and I try not to think of the life I left behind.

3

A DREAM GONE AND I AM STILL HERE, OR AM I?

I roll over and scrunch the blankets higher over my head. Is it morning already? It must be, as I hear little feet running back and forth, hungry tummies spilling cereal and almond milk on my new, clean kitchen floor. My bedroom window is slightly open. I stare for one second at my Victorian, floral curtains swaying in the gentle breeze. I take a slow, deep, grateful breath. Another day in my beautiful, easy life is about to begin. I have a lot to do, but there is nowhere I would rather be.

I am well rested; I feel totally safe; I feel love and peace all around me in a tangible, real way. My only worry is what I will feed this growing family for dinner tonight.

I am jolted back into the present. I look good today, as good as the 25-year-olds he hangs out with...*Wait, what is happening to my brain?* I love myself, and I don't compete with other women; I support them. *Where the hell am I?*

I was asleep, dreaming about my old life, how my family likes meat and potatoes and dessert and I never worry about the money I spend at the supermarket each week; I just get what I need, tossing in a lip gloss and gossip magazine here and there. Later, I sit on the sofa while dinner cooks; the whole house smells good. I am reading a good book and listening to my children run and play outside. I have nothing left to do; I already took a spin class today, and the kids have no activities tonight. I am my favorite thing: a mom.

"Wow, Candi, you scared me!" I jump out of the pages of my book, as my beautiful rescued lab mix jumps on the sofa next to me. She is a dream baby, has a big yard, a doggie door, food in her bowl, and the most loving heart. I have plenty in return to give her. She snuggles against me and actually smiles. I tell her she is a perfect angel. *We did it,* I think, *my first husband and I, we created the perfect life with so much to be grateful for. Wait, why am I not happy? I am not home. What is happening? Where am I?*

* * *

I CLOSE my eyes and feel the walls close in. I feel different, like the walls actually moved. It is a quiet shift, but I feel it. It feels like an eternity just passed me by. All at once, I am uncertain, cold, stressed, lost, alone. I just woke up, and I am exhausted beyond belief. I fully open my eyes, and the fog disappears. I know where I am now. I feel the weight; it is tremendous; it sinks me deeper. I have to be strong for my daughter. The flash of anger comes next; slow and steady, it fills me. I feel my dreams die. I smell my dog, but this is a different dog; he needs a bath, wants breakfast. Candi is gone, gone, and so is my dream life.

What the hell is poking me in the back? I know I am not home, and I know I live here. This house is too new, the colors all wrong, the windows too modern and too long. I see the beautiful backyard outside my window, the pine trees moving in the wind. I am so cold. My sick monster is here—no hug, no kiss, just sex, as he slips a piece of himself inside me and I accept, my body betraying me. I am not yet awake, but it is okay, easier not to fight him. I am trying so hard to keep the peace, working on my plan to get well and get out.

I remember too much all at once, and I cannot process it. Only my daughter is here, sleeping close by. My sons are an hour away at their dad's house. They are old enough to choose to live there. I had to let them go. I told myself that I did it for them. I should have fought for them. I wish I understood that they needed me. Instead, I wallow in my own pain. I will regret this until my last breath. Where is my life?

He roughly puts his hand in my hair, and I tell myself I like it. He forms a ponytail, pulls my head back, and slips inside me again. Well, good morning. I didn't even know he was in my bed, as we have our own rooms in his big house. I tell myself it feels good, but the truth is I would rather be anywhere but here, with him, touching me in the most intimate place without really touching me, seeing me, at all. So I close my eyes and dream of my escape.

4

HOW I GOT HERE

*I*t wasn't always like this, or maybe it was. When we first met it was amazing. Or maybe it wasn't. Maybe it was just new. I thought he was a natural leader, but now I know he just had money and was a bully. He doesn't take no for an answer from anyone. Ever. He easily turned all my noes into yeses. I didn't even have time to think about what I wanted; I just believed I wanted him.

* * *

LATER I FOUND out about love bombing and how they don't really care about you at all, going as far as mimicking your very own behavior, making you basically fall in love with yourself. He suddenly was a family man, he loved fitness—all of the things I did in my spare time he took an interest in. He would twist and repeat my own words to me, and I didn't even notice. The lie is invisible, the disguise of someone caring for you. You end up hating yourself after the lie is exposed. You feel stupid, used, devastated, that you didn't see; but this is the game they play, and they are masters at it. They don't have any genuine behavior, just an insatiable need to dominate, to own. The lie is complex, layered, never-ending. It is meant to confuse, consume. This is the monster of a narcissist. They don't ever care, they don't ever apologize or think they did anything wrong. You are left with just pieces of yourself, like distant memories. You have to muster all the strength you have ever had in your life, calling upon God to save you, as the damage and the look (for me, it was seven years) of pure evil is nothing you have ever seen before; and you were close, very close, inside.

If you don't understand this you are like I used to be. I would never have guessed this could happen to me. I let him in, I gave all—I wanted to, he allowed me to. I confused the lust I felt for him physically with love; he told me it was love, his words I so gullibly believed—"This is super love, I have never been in love before." I now live in his world, hell, until I find a way to escape. I fell for the phony version of himself that he gave me, and now I live with the monster. I gave up lifetime alimony just to be lied to. I left a man who loved me enough that I actually could have loved myself. I hurt my family, my children, but mostly myself.

I miss my old life, me. He has what he wants, and I have nothing. I gave up my job, my financial security, the only home I ever owned by myself, and, virtually, for a time anyway, my kids.

We "met" online; that is how you meet people as a single parent if you don't go to bars or want a one-night stand. I was divorced, in my own home, and bored and lonely. Yes, only three months after moving.

* * *

DESPERATE I WAS NOT. Having never really dated before, I literally went on at least twenty first dates. I met everyone in public, and no one got a second date. The block button became my best friend. Get a job, guys; post a real picture from this century. Jeeze. I gave no explanations—I was looking for **him,** right? I thought there was a one for me. Well, I met him alright. We met at a bar, for one drink; and, while he didn't quite look like the college picture he posted at his current age of 39, he kind of stopped me in my tracks—he crashed the fucking train. He called me while I was leaving the date, actually pulling out of the parking lot. I guess he found his easy target, and I wasn't getting away.

* * *

AFTER A FEW MONTHS, he meets my children; he is becoming a part of my life. I notice an awkward silence when it is anyone but just the two of us. This is the first red flag that I ignore. I don't really understand and think he is just quiet. Part of the plan is to isolate us fully from anyone and everyone that brings joy to our lives, and that he did. My brilliant longing for a compatible love, my amazing new talent to screw up my life, took away all of my ability to reason. This is not love. I let go of my own plans, my responsibilities, my future, and I let him in.

I keep telling myself over and over I am doing the right thing. He keeps telling me he is in "super love." I want my life to *start* already; I am tired of waiting. He had built his home, so I knew I would be moving one town over and into his life. I tell myself things like the school system is better than where I am. Later he says things to me like, "This can be our home, but it is **my** house." This will be in response to any little thing like me asking if I could put my wall unit against a wall. I give up control of my destiny to a man. I tell myself we are stronger as a family unit. Well, that is the biggest bullshit. I was a family to my kids. They had a wonderful father, too. It is fear; I let fear lead me. I became half of who I was, my confidence and my self-respect machine gunned by the monster.

Now I, Miranda Holmes, age 47, am the only one who can get my life back. I just hope it's not too late. Squashing everything inside of me, all the natural things I would do or say to deal with him, I have to placate the beast until I can finally get out of his house, out of this mess. I feel like he is a sick lion beast. I feed him, clean his house, do his laundry, take his darts. "What do you have against makeup?" he said one time when we were on line at the movies. I was just stunned. In the beginning, I told him, "Eat it," but then I had to deal with his devil of a temper. Growing up, I never thought I would be the kind of woman who would end up in an abusive relationship, and that is the thing: you don't know it is even happening.

My thoughts are confused. I tell myself, *Stay calm; I got this.* If I run again I am being impulsive, selfish, the same as before, not thinking about my children. I am thinking now. I am not safe anymore; I am not safe here if I am not thinking. I think, I plan, and I pray. He is growing bigger inside me, if this is even possible because he is already so big. It has been weeks, and my body wants to reject him as my mind orders, but it does not. Instead, I yield to him, accept him, arch my back, wish he would change.

He is heavily medicated for hair loss and has been on this medication for twenty years, so he cannot finish. He says it also helps him with his mood swings and rage issues. I shake my head, but it is still somehow good. He puts his arms around me, which is rare. I try hard not to feel it, to like it, but I fit perfectly into him, his arms, the color of the hair running up his body, his hands, the way he smells. I try to shut it off, be still. I need this so much more than sex. I deny myself, don't touch him back. I am frozen, in control. He does not notice. I do this to survive him. He is pretend, not real, and he likes 20-year-olds.

* * *

WHEN I FIRST LOOKED BACK, I thought I did not see what was happening. But I did. I just literally could not accept what I saw. He cheated and he lied, over and over—he even cried. I had no idea who he really was, or who he was not. He is no one, a sociopathic, malignant, narcissistic, soulless, evil creature. A man would not do that to a woman. I believe this still.

At the time, he fit into a role, a moment. I was vulnerable, confused, and a ridiculously easy target. He is not charming, not fun nor funny; he never laughs. Actually, when a sound comes out, he is usually making an evil kind of sneaky sound that leaves you wondering if there was something more you missed. He is a loner—literally has not a single friend, only employees or people who cheer him on or do his bidding because he loaned them money. His speech comes out in the form of an order, like he has the job of delegating what everyone should do all of the time. He demands and people follow and don't question. He is not my lover, not my friend, not my future. He is no longer my enemy because to beat him would be to walk alone in the darkness with no real winner anyway. His favorite meal is anger, and I will not feed him again. Right now, I just live here, with him. We eat together sometimes, have occasional, rough, unsatisfying sex; and he is happy. He thinks to himself how ideal this is: a live-in cheerleader, a maid, a slave. I am the longest relationship he has ever had, and I wonder how I have this honor. I stop myself from calling out terrible names in my head.

Jay and his dad own a construction company. They do government work and are busy and successful. He spends his long days yelling and fighting with his employees, the people who hire them, inspectors, attorneys, and even his dad. When we met, he convinced me my fitness jobs were shit and I could help him and make more money. I realized later it was just one more way to control every part of me, my finances as well.

I do research for his company, from home or anywhere I am. I find people, equipment, research cars, and run his fucking errands. I am sitting in the home office, just kind of zoning out from lack of sleep, when I suddenly hear too much silence. I am hyperaware even in my sleep. I realize I left the ringer on my phone on vibrate when I woke up and see I have eight missed calls from him. Fuck.

I stopped requesting he call just once and wait for my return call because he does not listen to a word I say. I have my phone with me everywhere, even in the bathroom. I tell myself it is just easier this way, but it owns me and breaks me and invades all of my peace. Sometimes he calls "just to say hi," but if I do not answer he yells at me. He is a freak, a total control freak. I work for him, so he knows exactly where I am!

* * *

WHEN WE FIRST STARTED DATING AND I was still normal, we were spending many weekends together before I knew how he really was, and I just wouldn't answer the phone if I was busy. He called too much, and sometimes I didn't feel like speaking. I should have seen the second red flag here because he would literally drive forty minutes to see where I was, even showing up at my sister's house if my car was there. Giant red fucking flag above his head. Didn't see it.

I wonder so intensely how I could have ever been drawn to him. Now that I know about his disorder it is easier to understand. He is pure evilness. He is cold, ice cold, has no compassion, no connection, empty eyes. I honestly believe he has no feelings, yet I am drawn to him. Even in my recovery, I still feel the pull sometimes. Each time we breakup and then he comes for me, I try to be reasonable with him, communicate, beg him to listen, start over. He talks me into telling myself he isn't so bad—"I actually married him, so he must be okay." I think I was in some sort of trance, having an internal battle. I tell myself that, even though he never wanted marriage, he did this for me. I ignore the fact that he is a terrible person, a terrible friend, a terrible human. It never felt like we were married, not even on our wedding day.

He altered the course of my life. My sons not being here…

nothing will ever be the same. I will pick up the shards of my heart and tape them back together, though. Freedom. I wonder if I am turned on by what I perceive to be his alpha-maleness.

The past keeps flashing before my eyes, the loss of everything that mattered, the actual things I always wanted, had…gone. The man who treated me like a queen…I actually was the happiest I had ever been to this day. He was a great friend, husband, co-parent, but I was just not happy with myself. I needed to grow up. I craved growth, change, movement, the walls to be freshened up, the lamps to be moved. Now I see the monster every day and see he is the opposite of what I had for fifteen years: mean, sick, demanding. "No" is never an option for him. But at the end of this road, there will not be another monster to fill this space. I will be the one to look in the mirror at my mistakes and my journey and to put my hands firmly on the wheel and drive the damn car myself, my way, alone.

5

OPEN YOUR EYES, STUPID

SOME SIGNS I WISH I TOOK SERIOUSLY:

He is a psychopathic, sociopathic, malignant narcissist. Period.

DOES NOT GET JOKES, GET OR EVEN REACT TO SARCASM:

The confusion of this relationship is immediate because if you are a good person, like I am, you just get so confused and keep trying. For example, he will laugh at himself, so you keep trying to connect with him, act normal. It isn't until later you realize he was asking you to stroke his enormous ego, that he doesn't care what you say or think about anyone or anything; he just wants you to cheer for him. It is empowering to see my anger die, and I become fascinated by this horror, this very real horror of at least what looks like a human being.

ENJOYS POKING FUN AT YOU IN FRONT OF OTHERS:

Again, he seems to have a long-running private joke with himself (creepy, yes); and he won't hesitate to make fun of any little thing about you, almost making it seem like an act, in front of others so they think he **is** connected in a normal way to you. This isolates you, because what your closest friends and family see prevents them from seeing and accepting what he actually is.

GETS ANGRY IF YOU HAVE A CHANGE IN MOOD OR BECOME QUIET:

After all the cruel treatment and the mind-numbing confusion and the demands of your time and attention, he immediately notices if you are upset or quiet. It must be the loss of control over you that makes him suddenly seem to care. Don't be fooled—he will use anything you tell him, anything you feel, against you later. He will turn your words against you in the form of criticism and verbal abuse.

"You should be the happiest person in the world—what is wrong with you? You ungrateful bitch, I cannot make you happy; I have done everything I can for you!" he has said these and much worse to me, not only damaging my body image and denting my confidence but causing me to be clinically depressed. This seems unforgivable, but that is what makes you stuck!!! Until you realize he will **not** validate your pain, clear up your confusion, or **ever love you back** you cannot move on. Take his power over you away; let it go and move on. It is that or the death of your soul. Please leave. This is not your fault in any way. He would tell me how to dress or to put more makeup on. He would say I was fat, and I could not see myself trying to please him, trying to change for him, or that this was a toxic and damaging relationship until I left.

EXPECTS YOU TO "LISTEN" TO HIM:

His word is law; he will not compromise in any way, for anyone, under any circumstance—even with the law. He may appear to say the right words to you, but that is only to get what he wants, to serve only his goal or purpose. This happens time and time again, and it takes a while to realize what is happening because if something bad is happening to YOU he will fight to the death, and this seems like he is on your side. He is not; he is never on your side. There is only and forever one side: his. He loves the fight; he enjoys the emotions and hurting others. This is his fuel. Read that again. Hurting you and others, instigating and bringing out emotions, even rage and danger—that is his fuel. That is why "no contact" and "Gray Rock" work. Take back your power; walk in the light. The Gray Rock Method is best described as having no response to these emotional vampires in any and all situations. In cases where there are shared children or other reasons to tolerate their presence, you have to always keep in mind that their game and their food and fuel is to lure us into using our emotions, so you must use all of your will to show none so they move on. It works, trust me. The simplest things they want power over. At one point, it felt like he was driving the car from the passenger seat. To survive, you have to obey—"turn here, pull over, stop the car"—you just do it. You are a puppet with no voice. Get out; run as fast as you can.

CARES NOTHING FOR YOUR NEEDS AND DOESN'T SEE YOU AS A PERSON BUT AS A POSSESSION:

If you are tired he doesn't care. If you are injured he doesn't care. My ex would actually send someone over from his job if I needed anything for myself or for the house; he never did anything for me himself.

HAS A LACK OF RESPONSE IN CONVERSATIONS:

THIS IS BIZARRE. You speak to someone of your day or children or feelings or the weather, and he just has no response. I got a blank stare every time I spoke, but he would ramble about things that mattered to him, usually material possessions or how he dominated at something or had a fight with someone. It is bizarre to be sitting in a car with someone and realize, over and over, they didn't hear a word you said.

NEVER BECOMES FAMILIAR WITH YOU:

Doesn't show affection or sometimes even acts like he doesn't know you. I have never hugged or been hugged by the man I was with for almost seven years. Once, I walked in the room while he was talking to someone, and he acted like he didn't know me—it was mind boggling.

EXPECTS YOU TO BE AT HIS BECK AND CALL:

If he wanted to go somewhere or, to be more accurate, to be driven somewhere, even at 9 pm, I was to be happy and agreeable at all times or deal with his temper.

NEVER TAKES RESPONSIBILITY FOR ANYTHING HE DID WRONG:

Bragging is a favorite pastime for these types of people, but don't expect him to admit he ever made a mistake. He will never admit, even to himself, he did something wrong. This is the lie, this is how you can see it, true narcissism.

HE THREATENS YOU:

Any little bit of confidence that appears in you, or any bit of trying to tell him to stop the abuse or that you will leave, starts with him insulting you and usually ends in violence. This happened to me over and over before I saw the cycle and his bullshit apologies. I had dozens of apologies on my phone at any given time. Never lose **your** temper with him, or you will see the monster up very close, and he will let you know he will take everything you have, including your reputation. He threatened to kill me if I fought him during our divorce, and I believed him.

HE IS A BAD ROLE MODEL, ESPECIALLY FOR CHILDREN:

My children, well, my sons, who only saw him once or twice a month, became impressed by this person. This was one of the hardest things I had to endure, as I am the reason they were exposed to him in the first place. They saw him as "fun" and, as young, ambitious men, saw him as a risk-taker.

HE WANTS PUBLIC SEX:

Even in the house, he always tried this, seeming to get off on getting caught by my kids!?!?!? That is truly disgusting and evil. He was constantly trying to do this—in the kitchen, in the garage, anywhere—and he always got mad at me for saying no, which consisted of dragging myself away while his strong hands were on my body, on my clothing, trying to rip them off of me.

HE WILL CALL UNTIL YOU ANSWER:

He is obsessed with power and control. He would call ten times and text me to call him until I did. He would always yell at me and accuse me of ignoring him if I did not answer right away. It was like a fucked up high school game. It became easier to answer. Now I will run my phone over.

* * *

REMEMBER, he cannot love you back. Once again, **he cannot love you back!** Remember, these people feel entitled, they feel empowered over all things, without conscience. The most empowering and important thing I can say to you, after almost seven years of living like this, is I finally, finally know when to stop talking to him. That doesn't mean that, while I am still in this house, I am not forced to have "yes" and "no" conversations with him—remember, if you ignore him or get mad you feed the monster—but to his nasty comments I can now say, "Just so you know, just so you aren't jealous, I was working late." I now have taken back almost all of my power. I am still here and I am human and I am honest with myself that it still hurts sometimes. I now have the power and ability to protect myself, to squash my instinct to defend myself like an adult. I know better than to say, "What are you talking about? I am not jealous. I didn't ask where you were. We signed divorce papers." I realize my instinctive ability and desire to communicate, to fix, to be understood, **will be wasted on this person and used against me.** So for now, I still have one eye open, because that is the secret: keep your power. No matter how long it takes for you to stop hurting, do not show it!!!

I had a good friend, a life coach, who somehow understood all of this, tell me that I had gone from being the victim to being the teacher. While I do not want validation from anyone at this time, this hit home. I have literally taken back my thoughts, my will, my power. I did not do it alone. Websites and a ton of reading not only educated me on these types of relationships and people (horrors) but made me feel understood, not alone, not crazy, less hurt, and even validated. I thank anyone who shares their pain, in stories, in quotes—it matters. You helped me and you matter.

* * *

I WANT to touch on something else here: the doubt. The doubt that will creep in must be contained. You must control your thoughts here at this critical transition time when you must speak to him if he calls you about work or something mundane. Due to circumstances after we signed divorce papers, I was still living in the house for a month while my daughter finished school before I could implement "no contact." Although he might make a rude or negative or critical comment, I had to squash my normal need to respond. Remember, he is looking to feed. Do not become his fuel. For example, not answering the phone while I still lived there would fuel him, give him pain and anger and emotion. He is fueled by emotions, especially feeling powerful over you. He cannot and does not see you as a person. My two points would be to watch out for **confusion** and **time spent thinking** about him or a situation that happened or something he said. I found myself questioning things all the time, *Is he a narcissist? Is it me? Am I the problem? Am I needy? Am I jealous?* This is what helped me realize that none of this was my fault, none of this was in my head, and he *did this to me.*

Remember the flags: one, I was always confused, always recounting words and conversations, wondering what the hell was happening. The second flag was the amount of time I spent trying to figure out what was going on, evaluating this. I look now at the time that was stolen from me. So much time stolen from my kids. So much time went by, and nothing ever got resolved, and I was always on my toes, always very confused. This is a man who physically and verbally abused me for years, who lied to me daily, and who cheated on me with no remorse, more than once. This treatment was so foreign to me, as I would have never treated anyone this way. He took pieces of me. And while I was down, at my worst, a good person, a mother, he kept kicking. So to look back now and see how messed up that is…well, it leaves me speechless. We are survivors. He wanted me dead. There is no other explanation.

* * *

MELISSA M. SACHS

"He Can't Love You Back"

He took me,
He took me in.
He told me lies;
I died within.
He took me;
He told me yes.
How he was I couldn't have guessed.
I gave and gave,
I smiled, I planned;
And then I lost; he's not a man
But a devil with no soul
To dominate and crush the goal.

CHORUS:
I can't even hate him or he will see—
No one understands how sick and mean.
He took all the good inside
And made me small; I almost died.
He crushed my dream.
I want to scream it to the world—
All the boys and all the girls,
Run, run or you will crack;
What you see isn't what you get.
He can't, he can't love you back.
He touched me; I didn't see.
He touched me; it wasn't me.
He took me then dragged me down.
He blamed me; he ate my crown.
I wanted him; I tried so hard—
I didn't know he has no heart.
The dream is over—
Just pain and pieces to pick up now.

No four leaf clover; more lies abound.
I signed the papers and heard his threats;
I am almost free, just not yet.
The day will come when you will see...
Oh wait, he can't, he can't love me.

CHORUS:
    I can't even hate him or he will see;
    No one gets it unless like me.
    They take the good, the good inside;
    They don't care if you die.
    I want to scream it to the world—
    Every boy and every girl,
    Run, run or you will crack; he can never
    Love you back.

HE TOOK ME, he took me in with lies;
    He took me by force to my surprise.
    He took me, took me inside;
    He told me yes then he watched me die.
    How he was never could have guessed.
    I gave, I gave; he made me less.
    I smiled, I planned but then I lost,
    Never knowing this love
    Would have a cost.
    I loved him despite his goal.
    He took me, almost my soul.
    I woke up and I'm not me.
    He's a devil, not the man you see.

CHORUS:

MELISSA M. SACHS

Can't hate him or he will see;
Protect yourself or you won't be.
I want to scream it to the world—
All the boys and all the girls,
Run away and don't look back;
He will never love you back.

WRITTEN BY: Melissa Sachs

6

A SLOW DEATH BUT STILL TRYING TO MAKE IT WORK

I wake up as the morning light sneaks through my closed eyes, which I want to keep closed, and I try to block out the sound: his large, gross feet coming down the hall, sliding and dragging with each step. He walks toward the bathroom, right next to my room. I hold my breath. He chooses the shower instead of my room. I breathe.

I am going to visit Candi today. My old dog, the perfect, smiling lab mix I had to give away. I gave her to a nurse and her family. They said they would provide foster care while I got my shit together. They, of course, now want to keep her. The dad is retired, religious, kind. They have another dog, too; and they are like the family I used to have, used to be. During one of my horrific breakups with Jay, after I actually sold my own home to live with him, I ended up renting an apartment next to my sister briefly, thinking we would work it out, thinking it was just a bad fight, he was really mean sometimes but still normal—little did I know at the time. The apartment I rented did not allow dogs, but my sister had a nice yard ten feet from me and said she would keep my dog until I figured it out. I was still taking care of her needs; she just couldn't sleep at my place. Suddenly, my sister's husband got very sick, and for several weeks, they didn't even tell me it was because he is allergic to dogs.

My sister worked with the nurse who agreed to foster her, her dog falling in love with mine, me losing even more. I just kind of approved, feeling lost. I did ask Jay to help me, and his one word answer, as I will never forget to this day, was, "Never." I have visited her many times, secretly asking her if she was okay, but I can see how happy she is. She sleeps in their bed because she is an angel and they love her so much. They send me Christmas cards thanking *me* for allowing them to keep her. She is my dog. I miss her and I dream about her and I cry alone. Time does not change how I feel. No amount of time, not other dogs, nothing. I fucked up. The good news is she is happy and loved. The bad news is I can add that choice to my ever growing list of mistakes that hurt me and my children.

* * *

I NOW LIVE WITH HIM. I have since adopted another dog because the kids talked me into it and, well, we love dogs. He is a small male lab mix, and he is an angel, too. He is sweet and loving and stinky. Jay, the monster, got him a doggie door and an electric fence. He only did this because he thought I worry too much about getting home to the dog. I will be more available to do his bidding and stay out longer if the dog can let himself out to be alone instead of being alone inside. So now I have another dog that I take care of by myself, as my sons are only here on occasion and my daughter is usually hiding in her room away from Jay.

"What? Let me guess—you want to go home because of the dog?" I often hear him say. I think quietly to myself, *No, asshole, I am just tired.* I named him Pup. The pound named him Bear, but you just don't call that out when you live in Pennsylvania. There are bear everywhere!

My Pup looks at Jay for approval; no matter how many kisses I give him and how much I play with him, he notices that Jay does not notice him. I watch in mixed horror and fascination, admiring Pup's determination and never-give-up attitude. He just quietly waits for the monster to notice him, breaking my heart a little. Another flag, a big one, too. I assumed he just didn't like dogs, but I see now it is fucking odd as hell.

One day, Jay put his hand on Pup's back, as he always lay next to him. He did not move, did not stroke his shining black fur; he just laid his big hand there. I could see my calm, quiet, well-behaved dog's shock. He eyes opened wide, and he did not move, but he was happy.

I tell myself in these moments I do not hate Jay, do not hate this relationship, that everyone is different. But he never shows me affection, none, ever. Sometimes I tell myself this makes it easier; I can be me, not be a part of him. But that is always a lie. I want more, even a quarter of what I have to give, but I get none. I get less than nothing.

* * *

I WAKE up in a kind of fog each day, in his world, his house, use his car, work for him. I cannot always seem to find myself, but I am always looking. I realize I am with someone who plays me hard. He portrays himself as someone else, love bombing me blind; but he is no one, with nothing to share, not his life or his feelings. Money is his wife.

I struggle with the need to find a shred of good in him, anywhere, just a piece, a drop, so I don't have to end another marriage and my life doesn't have to be turned upside down again. I don't want to see what is right the hell in front of me, and know I need to escape this literal hell. Good, normal people like me look for a reason. I have a need to figure this out, yearn for closure, but there never will be. The realization that he is not, in any way, the person he presents himself to be is the whole problem. It creates confusion, lack of confidence, depression, and pain. I should **RUN!**

He turns on me in the blink of an eye if I forget or let go of my vigilance for even one minute. When this happens, I don't automatically think, *Wow, I am in an abusive relationship.* It took me years. One second, we would be eating dinner, and the next second, I might say something innocent that I think is funny but he thinks is sarcastic, and then he changes. His face changes—it's like a snap of the fingers and the lines on his face change. His eyes, unseeing and hard, become crazed. Fear is a tangible thing in the room; it permeates the air all around us. It is so real and so sudden, I have no time to wonder how, no time to react. I just need to fix it.

Once, we were fighting, and I said something he didn't like. The next thing I knew, my back was against the wall, and his hands were around my neck. Shock is not the right word. Again, you don't think, *Wow, I am in a verbally and physically abusive relationship.* You just think about how to make it stop in that moment, to survive it. His big hands around my neck, the air slightly knocked out of me, the fear massive, and all I could see were his eyes and his even more frightening teeth. He literally growled at me through his teeth, and I could hear myself saying "I'm sorry," while wondering if that was me speaking.

* * *

I REMEMBER JUST YESTERDAY READING an article in a trashy magazine about a celebrity who "got away" from an abusive boyfriend. She hid it from everyone, made them both look good, normal. He choked her, threw her against the wall, called her names. This is in a magazine? This is my life!

* * *

Eventually, he calms down, like a rabid dog that has been treated. But the vacancy never leaves his face, and his lame apologies are laced with blame—"I am sorry, but you shouldn't have said that to me." I stay fucking calm as hell, grateful my kids aren't seeing this, and plan another escape. I must get out. I start crunching numbers in my brain and hear my voice telling me he controls everything. I will need help. I am not safe here. My cell rings, and it is one of my boys. I take a millisecond to compose myself so my son cannot hear the anguish in my voice. My children see too much without knowing, as they are good and not evil, too young to understand. I have to hide it, to protect them. My kids think they like him. This kills me.

 I get at least three more texts the next day saying how sorry he is. I say that it is alright because I have no other choice. I need to keep the peace. The times I try to talk to him, to leave peacefully, he laughs in my face, tells me I made a deal with the devil...and that he loves me.

7

INSTEAD OF LEAVING I GET MARRIED: LIVING THE TRAUMA BOND AND CO-DEPENDENCY

*I*t's morning again. I am so cold, or maybe I am just afraid and the fear makes me cold. I pull the blankets over my ears and pull my knees up closer to my chest. Something has changed, or maybe I just care less and wish it to be true. Time has gone by. I have come to an almost peace to get through my day-to-day, like a zombie. I do this to keep my sanity, to focus on my kids. This peace makes him believe I am happy, I will stay, he has me—in his words, "I own you." He talks about buying me a ring. My thoughts do battle... one thought: *I need to stay in one place and have security;* next thought: *I will never have security as long as I am with him.* I forget sometimes that I actually despise him, hate being here, hate living with him in this bullshit half-life.

I have an underlying anger—I hold it deep inside for now—for what he is, for what he did, for what he does, for what he is not. As time goes by, I appear to evolve into someone who does not give a shit. I gave him all of me, and now I can't figure out how or find the strength to get some back.

* * *

I REMEMBER the first time it happened, the very first moment I did it, felt it, when I took the love I had for myself out and away from me and put it into someone else. The dreams, the goals, the very plans I had for my life I gave to another person so I didn't have to hold them, to use them or be responsible for them.

His name was Glen; I was 16 years old. I gave him my feelings, my heart, my dreams, and the responsibility to own them. I did all of this subconsciously, of course, because I was insecure and afraid. Because it was easier to love someone else, instead of myself.

I was a typical latch-key kid. I woke up by myself, went to school, washed my own clothes, cleaned the house, worked at 12 years old. I sometimes made crappy dinners for my younger sister. My mom worked and went to school. My dad lived in a different state, and we had nothing. No one ever checked my homework, or me, but somehow I made it through high school. I told myself later it was because I was smart—hardly opened a book, studied in homeroom before each test—but the teachers saw I was well behaved and poor with no involved parents, so they probably just passed me. No one cared if I got an A or a D, so neither did I. Besides being the middle child who was agreeable and helpful, I basically did whatever I wanted to. I am thankful I was never tempted by drugs or got caught up in the wrong crowd. My mother was alone for many years, and with three daughters, she was very short-tempered and very stressed. My father broke her heart, and for as long as I could remember, she wore her pain like an angry badge, like permission to be mean and critical of everyone, especially her own kids. We didn't clash much because I was never there or she was never there, but I do remember one fight in particular. I don't even remember what it was about; I just remember she threw a book at me from across the table. I never raised my voice to her as I was afraid of her and always tried to walk the dog and have the house clean before she came home. I was certainly never violent toward her, or towards anyone for that matter. I could feel the bruise forming on my chest.

It was freezing out that night, snow lightly falling, too. We lived in a condominium complex in Sussex County, New Jersey, with her boyfriend, who drank vodka on ice at all hours of the night, sometimes on the couch in my bedroom. It was the 1980s, a magical time, but of course, we had no magical cell phones back then. I was pretty upset, my mother having moved on to something else already, not giving me a second thought. I grabbed my coat and quietly left the house; no one noticed. I felt instantly free—and freezing, the kind of cold that makes your teeth chatter and your neck freeze through your jacket. I headed to the end of the street, which formed a circle leading to the community clubhouse. It was closed, but I was going to the payphone right out front.

I had met a boy a few months ago. It was teen night at a local dance club. My friend Trisha and I loved to dance, and she had a reliable car, so we usually went every week. We were drinking sodas and shaking to the music—they played the best music—the lights were dim...I loved it there. I was singing out loud when he got the nerve to walk up to me. The dance floor was full, teen to teen. As I leaned against the bar, there was innocence and laughter all around, arms rubbing against each other. His smile was adorable; his hair, blonde. I saw nothing fake there and felt my stomach do a little flip as he smiled and looked right at me and said, "You should be dancing. Would you like to dance?"

He sounded nervous and brave, so I said, "Sure," which is funny because I was so shy around boys and had never dated one before. I was 16 years old. He told me his name was Glen. I looked up and saw Trisha dancing with his friend, and we had a great time. I saw Trisha give the other boy, Tom, her number, and I quickly said goodbye and dashed out of the place. I kind of ran, turning my back on him. I wasn't really interested and laughed the whole way home while my friend told me how in love she was.

The following weekend, I rode my bike eight miles to her house as I often did. Once trapped and thirsty, she told me Tom and his friend were coming over. I wasn't even sure it would be Glen, and I was just an innocent girl going with the flow. They were two years older than us, seniors at a high school about thirty miles away. They pulled up in their Camaro—this was cool and scary to me at the same time—and it was him. He confidently walked up the stairs and said "Allison, it's you!"

This immediately put me at ease, and I laughed and said "Who is Allison?" He thought I was joking, but he had heard me wrong at the club. I kept telling him my name was Miranda, and he still didn't believe me, thinking I gave a fake name.

We started hanging out, and we took long drives and ate pizza. We eventually exchanged numbers, and while I didn't let him kiss me yet, I could feel myself starting to have feelings for him. Glen ended up being the only boy I dated in high school, my first kiss, my first everything.

I was shivering as my cold fingers slid the coin into the slot on the cold silver phone. He answered on the second ring. "Hello?" he said.

"Hi, it's me, Mandy!" He sounded so happy to hear from me that I instantly filled with emotion and relief that calling him was the right thing to do. I felt safe, like I was not alone anymore. His deep voice was so sexy, inviting, accepting. I felt less lost and like I was a part of something. He was so real, so cool to me and so sweet. My first boyfriend, my angel.

"I had a fight with my mom, and she threw a book at me. I hate my life," I said. It all rushed out at once. I could not be strong anymore; I could not stop the tears, the pain. I felt so unloved, neglected, unhappy.

He was compassionate for an 18 year old. He listened; he cared. His parents were divorced, too. We talked for a few more minutes, promising to see each other on the weekend, and we were about to hang up when he said one more thing. I can still hear his voice, the exact breath he took, the exact words, the honesty of it, the way he paused. He was brave. He wanted me to know.

"Mandy, I love you."

So simple, so direct, honest, heartfelt, and so powerful. I did not use these words in my life unless, maybe, I was talking to my dog. I was shocked, silent. I could not believe he just said that. It had never, ever occurred to me that he felt that. He then said, "You don't have to say anything." The time ran out on the phone, and the line went dead.

I stood there, cold phone in hand, snow falling, mixing with my tears. Just like that, all of my anger was gone. Just like that, I knew I loved him back, that I was now a part of his life, that I had a partner. I honestly loved him with my whole heart. I loved him too much. I was so young and inexperienced, but we lasted for four years. It was pure and beautiful. I would have married him, no doubt in my mind, but his college plans and life got in the way. We could not make it work as I always needed more of him. I chose him, chose love, over everything else, over me. It was the first time I made that mistake, forgot about myself, my own plans, my future. I gave the monster all of myself. Thirty-one years later, I find myself on the same road to recovery. The difference this time is I will own my own behavior. If I get out of this alive I will not repeat the same mistakes. But first, I got married…

8

TIME WARP

I roll over, scrunch the blankets higher over my head. I wear socks to bed now, but my feet are still cold. My bear, Pup, jumps on my bed. He is warm and sweet, a furry ball of heat wanting me to get up and give him his breakfast. I put my legs close to his warm little body, and he waits patiently.

I tell myself today is a new day, but the truth is I wake up tired again, tired of trying, tired of trying to be positive, to figure it all out. I yield to my monster, his needs, his demands. I don't even know my own desires because I work so hard to keep the peace, to keep him happy, that I can hardly recognize myself anymore. My need for calm, for sanity, is so strong that I only think of his needs and don't even know I am doing this. I always do what he wants.

By yielding, I sometimes think I see small changes in him, but a bigger piece of me is falling off in order for me to try to make this work.

I am in my home office, missing my sons today. They barely gave PA a chance. Their dad's "yes" to come back to NJ was a "no" to me. My pain of missing them, being with them daily, never decreases. I cannot financially afford to move back; this helps me talk myself into staying with the monster. He lied, he distracted me. I blame him; **he is** to blame for my sons leaving. They are healthy, smart, beautiful kids, and nothing makes me miss them less.

I just checked my weekly lottery tickets: "Not a winner." Am I optimistic or insane to think I can be free of Jay? The days turn into weeks, turn into months, turn into years, and I am still here, in some sort of trance, looking at cheap wedding dresses.

9

THE LION AND HIS LION BLANKET

I wake up, and it is still dark outside. I feel warm today for a change. There is this guy in Wilkes Barre, Pennsylvania, who sells these amazing blankets on the corner of the highway. They wrap you in and heat you up in this velvet-like material. One year, we bought everyone a blanket for Christmas; they all went crazy over them. Jay has bought no less than twenty of these for himself over the last two years. I have two on my bed, and each of the kids has one in both PA and NJ. We call them "lion" blankets. The first one he bought had this huge, beautiful picture of a tiger on it, and I guess he thought it was a lion. I love these damn blankets—they hug you. I wrap my feet in the bottom.

* * *

W<small>HEN</small> we first started spending weekends together at my place, he would actually bring his own lion blanket when he came over —he did not want to share. And if we had a fight, which was often in the beginning, he would call me to let me know he was coming over to pick up his blanket. He would knock on the door, and I would hand him the just washed blanket and shut the door in his face.

Now that we are living together, we have separate rooms and blankets in all of them and some on the couch and in the closets, too. Last night, he came down to my bedroom, while eating cookies and slurping sugary iced tea, and he laid his head across my stomach. I swallowed my thoughts of *Get the fuck off me*.

When I ignorantly believed he liked me and I was, well, madly in love with him and he kissed me, I mean really kissed me, it was amazing. That was the first year, and it has been two whole years since he kissed me like that. I think if he tried to kiss me now I would bite his tongue off and spit it in his face, but I hide this thought, too. When he was done with his cookies, he leaned in for a "kiss" goodnight, which consisted of him squeezing his eyes shut and a closed-mouth peck. He seemed happy, like we had kissed or something. But he is a liar, a fraud, a crook. Kissing me with his eyes shut, holding his hand on his shirt so it doesn't touch the dog. I stopped pretending to care but smiled anyway to avoid his wrath. He had a snake-like, cookie-filled mouth that I no longer had the desire to kiss. At all. I…really…didn't!

* * *

OF COURSE, not being a doctor or counselor of any kind, I have no idea how sick he is, that he has OCD, that he is a violent narcissist. At first, it feels like rejection, and I let it just eat at me. Like any normal person, I try to discuss this with him, but his bizarre answers make me stop trying. He says the meds he is on reduce his sex drive, and he is afraid to get too close to me because he thinks I might leave again. Both true! He can never communicate in the way I need which is to solve the problem. His needs are first; his answers are final.

Time just keeps going by, and I don't see yet that I am going crazy. I feel well rested today. My beautiful daughter sleeps like an angel in her rose-painted room with the new chandelier over her bed. I am aware I am fooling him for the most part, fooling everyone, almost fooling myself. I am agreeable, peaceful, grateful. I work Sundays for him now, too. "Sure, whatever you need," I say. I know I am trapped, but I plan my escape daily anyway. I just need one thing to go right, one thing to work out. I am stuck, like the Band-Aid on my thumb from this papercut that won't heal. It keeps sliding as I work, ripping off more skin each time I take it off, the area around the cut, raw, red, angry. It wants to heal, but it just needs a bit more time. I calm myself down, tell myself there is time to get it right; another year won't kill me. In my weak moments I try, again, to discuss this with him, tell him we are both stuck, unable to move forward, that we should end it peacefully, support each other. He tells me I am an ungrateful bitch and I can never make it on my own. For years, I don't even realize this is abuse. He pulls me into the bathroom and forces sex on me, never noticing I am not moving or responding in any way. He really is having sex with himself. I am just a possession.

My feelings begin to burn. I feel real rage, but I am in total control. I am more powerful now because I can hold my rage in, aim it, keep it until I am ready. I tell myself to be strong, that I didn't know he was like this, that he hid it. That giving up my own home, my own business, my own car, that moving into his empty life where he controls everyone and everything isn't my fault. I didn't know. I believe in love, and it bites me in the ass—hard. I am going to stay calm, plan, and leave. But then things get worse.

10

WHAT TRUST?

*T*rust is an odd thing. People have strong opinions until they experience the heart-wrenching rip in their soul when someone abuses their trust. When you lose trust it changes you. You are not expecting it to be like this, to have this insecure pain of wondering steal your time. For me, in this instance, it causes me to never feel safe again, to never feel sure again. Ever.

You grow up hearing and believing that "trust is earned" and the opposite, "trust is blind;" but depending on what experiences you have in life—and I can tell you, from much experience now—both are true. Trust **is** earned. If you don't know someone they can prove to you that they are trustworthy by their actions over time in different situations. If you do know someone then you usually, subconsciously, blindly trust them, until they prove otherwise.

* * *

GOING INTO THIS RELATIONSHIP, if you can call it that, I had ignorant, blind, total trust. I trusted his words mostly. I trusted and believed, without any doubt, when he said he loved me. I literally just assumed he was trustworthy. Looking back, I suppose I just wanted it to be true. I think this fact made the hit of finding out he was with other women every single chance he got ten times worse for me. I was not prepared in any way to handle or accept this behavior, and along with the searing pain was this kind of stunned embarrassment that it happened to me.

The first woman I found out about was 26 years old. Her name was Shantell. It sounded like a stripper's name, and I found out later she was referred to as the town whore. During one of our bigger fights, when I did not see him for almost three weeks, he was with her. He later said, "My dad was talking to her," at one of their jobs, so that was his excuse for having sex with her for three weeks. Now, he did not admit this to me until *after* we were married, and I chose to ignore what was right in front of me. He called me; he asked me to come back to him, not the other way around. Whenever he came back for me, he came back so hard that I was immediately unable to think, to process, to stop myself from going. I really thought he missed me, loved me. I had no idea his young whore had up and left him and I was always his fall back, his second choice.

I actually told myself that I was better with him, my kids liked him, and that he loved me, too. Next thing I knew, I was texting him back, taking his calls, defending him to my sister, and putting my things in his truck. I found out about all of his indiscretions after we were married. My whole world was shattered, my confidence, too. He always had a story, and he always said, "Well, if you didn't leave me it would never have happened."

By then, my daughter was in school in his town and I had a ring on my finger. He just kept saying that I never should have left, and I just kept thinking that I never should have come back. He seemed to enjoy my pain, as if he were punishing me. I had never witnessed nor experienced this type of abuse before, and I had no idea what was happening to me. Time just sort of froze for me then.

11

COMA

It is morning already. I strain to hear the sound over my fan. Is it him walking down the hall? I feel outside of my body, losing all trust for the first time in my life. I constantly battle myself to move on and ignore it or to find out more, to find out the truth. He, the only person who could, won't help me. Stomp, stomp, slide—he is coming. Slam, he walks into the bathroom, turns on the shower, and I praise the Lord. He has a huge bathroom in his room, but during one of our fights, he kicked the shower wall down. We were fighting over her. For two whole years, he never explained what happened; he never apologized for hurting me, for lying to me; he never felt regret. I will never forgive him. I just wanted the truth. I never blamed her. It just blew my mind that he was with her, here, in this house he asked me to live in with him. I asked him, over and over, to just explain it to me, but he just called me names and told me to let go of the past. I could not, and things got worse.

12

NOT MY NORMAL

I woke up with a terrible headache this morning, my lion blanket hanging off the bed, my feet freezing. I could hear him blowing his nose in the shower, over and over, the steam releasing his congestion and him just letting it fly. I resent everything about him now. I am so sick of cleaning up his nose shit. He disgusts me, and this disgust gives me some sort of relief.

Most days, I am clear on my mission: save money, leave. Simple, right? He opens my bedroom door after his shower. He smells of cheap cologne and hair gel. He proceeds to tell me what a great sleep he had. He does not look at me, see my distress, my headache, my heartache; he just sees himself. "I feel great!" he says, then asks me if I like his new shirt. I think to myself, *He is a total moron.* I wonder how I ever let him into my life but smile and say, "Yes, you look great." During the day, he stops at home to say his shirt is too tight and is bothering him, so he changes and leaves the shirt on the floor.

I still have a raging headache and want nothing more than a second hot shower and to wipe the look off my face before he sees it, but it is too late. "You look flustered," he mumbles. He looks at me like I am a bug he is trying to understand or dissect.

I force a smile; it is getting harder to look at him, now that I see. I squint at him and form a crinkly curve with my lips, while wishing him dead, and say, "No, I am okay. I was just going to take a shower, unless you need anything," (like to shovel more shit into my life).

* * *

IT IS the same each day with him: After hours of research, I make dinner he does not like, spend time with my daughter, and go to bed. I picked up Mexican tonight, so dinner is ready. I decide to jump in the shower before he comes home, using the hot water as a form of meditation that lasts for a minute or so. I see my phone needs to be charged, so instead of taking it into the bathroom with me, I plug it in. I decide to take a bath instead, as my back hurts. I am so stressed that I get in with barely an inch of water. Everything inside and outside of me hurts, and my thoughts are almost always about what a piece of shit and liar he is and what he has done to my life, to my brain. I find myself wondering where he really is. This is part of the loss of trust. It consumes me. I wonder who he is speaking to right now, why I care, and if he gave me an STD. I look at Facebook® photos of "her," try to understand, hope she has a boyfriend.

I breathe deeply and ask God for help. I hear my angel child singing while she eats her tacos. I get out, dry off, and wait for divine inspiration, believing it will come. I force myself to remain open, be positive, so I do not miss it when it arrives.

I throw my clothes on, my skin still wet, grab my slightly charged phone, go sit outside and watch my dog play. This whole process lasted less than fifteen minutes, but I see he called twice in the last ten minutes. I wish I could run over my phone so he could never call again. Nine out of ten times when I call him he does not answer, always saying he either missed my call or was on the other line. I quickly text him that my phone was charging while I was in the shower. I am home at the same time each day; he knows exactly where I am. He does not respond to my text or call me back, and a shiver runs up my spine as he pulls into the driveway. He walks up the three steps and stands in front of my chair and asks, "Are you mad at me." It was a statement not a question. "I see you have your phone there but did not answer when I called," he says.

"Oh, I just texted you—I was in the shower," I squeak out, thinking what a psycho he is. I feel the entire world slow down. "I never got a text," he quietly states, but I see the monster just under the surface; I see his sickness. I proceed to show him the time he called, the time I responded, and then he notices a text from me on his phone. I fight the urge to punch him in the face, grab my child and dog, and run. He is sick. He just stares at me again, and I see nothing and wonder just what that hair drug he has been taking for twenty years is really doing to him. He often blames his rage on this. I see no articulate thoughts. He looks empty, hollow, except for the edges around his eyes. A tiny crinkle at the edge reveals his inner rage. I can see it.

I instinctively know that if I incite his temper now things will not go well for me. That he will not be able to control any part of himself. "Come inside," I say, "You must be hungry." He follows me inside, and I see him looking at me from the corner of his eye, almost like I am the monster, suspicious, like I did something wrong. I know this is too close, that I have to make a move soon, before this becomes my normal. Placating the beast cannot be my life. *I stayed five more years.*

13

TIME WARP TWO

It is morning again. I am in some sort of time warp; I can't remember yesterday, and then it is morning again. I sleep well despite the cold and the monster I live with. He is in the shower. I know soon he will say, "Good morning, how do I look?" but instead he asks, "Are you feeling better?" like there is something wrong with **me**!

"Yes," I say, smile, peck. I drop my daughter off at school, savor every sip of my coffee with mocha from Starbucks®. Once at my computer, I find things to do for him to keep myself busy while still being hyperaware of him pulling up, walking in. In an entire day I may see him for five minutes, but I wait, my guard always up. I keep the window slightly open so I can hear, be ready. I long for the day, minute, second, I can be away from him, never ever see him again, never make him dinner, answer his calls, wash his balled up socks.

I remind myself I made the choice to be with him, ask myself for forgiveness, believe I have been punished enough. Depression hits me like a ton of bricks today, the farce taking its toll. I envision myself in a little white house, in my future, a small window over the kitchen sink, lace curtains on the window, and a radio playing low as a teapot boils water on the stove. Just thinking this is possible makes me smile.

I wake up; it's 4:30 a.m. I am calm and shaking all at once. Today is the day—I am tired of waiting, of being afraid. It will never be perfect, so I am going. I must keep the urgency of it hidden for a little bit longer. I have to say goodbye to him as he leaves for the day without a drop of suspicion in the air. I have to drop my daughter off at school, act normal. I have to look him in the eye and be wide open while hiding. I can smell my own fear. I feel this weird burning sensation in the back of my throat; it travels all the way down to my stomach. I did it! I saved ten thousand dollars, rented a U-Haul, and am putting my plan into action today. Pray for me. I will be free soon.

I am home now, a nervous wreck. He does not call. The depth of my fear starts to become bigger than what I am able to carry, to hide, to bear. I feel the toll of these last few years weighing heavily on me. I remind myself that my feelings of guilt are a result of the abuse. I did try to communicate with him, to tell him, be honest. I tried to explain and be peaceful, even take the blame, but each time has ended the same, in violence. He takes my things from me, throws my belongings away, takes my car, but I never end up leaving. Later I'm suffocated by his apologies.

Will he stop by the house today? *No*, I tell myself, he almost never stops by the house. I reached out to my sisters yesterday, at the last minute, making sure I wouldn't lose my nerve, knowing I could not do it alone. I begged for help. It was a literal cry for help. They hate him. They blame me for staying, don't understand. But they come, two of them with trucks. They are skeptical, but they are here. They walk into this big, beautiful house they never visit and are so happy I am leaving. They call him rude, antisocial, see him as the one who changed me. They don't understand, but I don't care right now. I am in survival mode. They have no idea what he would do if he came home to find them here. "Hurry," I implore.

We throw my twenty-year-old china into cheap boxes, loosely wrapped in scattered paper towels. I must not do anything to alert him beforehand. I load my kids' scrapbooks from their pasts into the car as fast as I can and throw my daughter's and my clothes into large black garbage bags and toss them in, too. My fear is tangible. It pisses me off, but it drives me, too. My daughter, playing at school, has no idea we are leaving today and that she will change schools again. But we are going "home" today. I rented a tiny, gross apartment right near her dad and brothers. I must remember to leave a space for her in the truck.

I toss her precious tea sets into crates, place towels on top, hope they make it. I am running now, my heart racing hard, my family throwing my things into the backs of their cars, my brother-in-law generously taking two beds apart, out of breath. We don't speak as, somehow, they sense the importance of getting it done and getting out quickly. I take only what is mine, what is necessary. Last time I left, he threw out whatever I left behind, and it was a lot. In the midst of my fear I see my family; we work as a team. They answered my 911, my distress call, and I am eternally grateful.

Several months before, we had had a nasty fight. He was very rough, in front of me at lightning speed, my back against the wall, his hands around my neck.

"C'mon, we have enough," I say to my family, "let's go." I can feel him coming. My cell phone rings, and time stops. I can taste my freedom this time, so close, just past the driveway. If he comes he will stop at nothing to stop me, and if he can't stop me he will take my things, block the driveway, call the police.

"Hello?" I say, forcing myself to take a breath, noticing my family is instantly quiet, not breathing either.

"Hey," he says, "just checking in." He sounds suspicious.

I tell him I am good, just reading and chilling out, about to get on the treadmill. I tell myself to stop talking. "Hey, sorry I was so mean yesterday. I don't know how that happens, and you know I don't mean it."

I pretend I know what he is talking about and say, "It's okay," when I want to scream, "Fuck you!"

He says "Let's eat out tonight!" I tell him, "Yes, that sounds great," and we hang up.

Adrenaline rushes through my veins like fire. *He knows,* I tell myself over and over, out of breath. I see my family staring at me with mixed disgust and pity as I say goodbye to the furniture I have acquired over many years, that now decorates his house, providing the only warmth here, and I walk through the door without looking back. I yell my dog's name, and we are off.

My new apartment is awful; my sons won't even come over. I spend a lot of time at my ex-husband's house, cleaning my sons' rooms, doing laundry, making dinner. I feel so safe here. The slight discomfort I feel around him is always less than the joy to all be together. He thanks me when I leave and tells me I am always welcome.

* * *

WITHIN TWO WEEKS, he was parking outside my place every day, convincing my sons he was sorry; and they told me I should go back, that he was our family. He said all the right things, paid my rent, gave me back my car, and talked me into coming back. He sent two of his workers to collect all of my belongings. I never quite knew how he did this. My daughter only missed a few days of school, so I got her right back in. He had his attorney threaten to kill everyone in the building if I did not get my money back. And then, I was right back where I started. I told myself that I didn't want to struggle or change my daughter's school or even leave PA. I also told myself that I loved this man and was not ready to give him up.

14

YET ANOTHER FAILED ATTEMPT TO LEAVE

A few months later and things got even worse. I woke up and I didn't care about the damn lion blanket. He moaned several times in the shower as the hot water hit his back. I puked in my own throat. The night before, we had another fight. As I get stronger, I can tolerate less and less from him. I don't even know what it was about…maybe I stopped kissing his ass for two seconds, maybe he didn't like the tone of my voice.

One minute, we were driving to dinner—he wanted to go out to eat every single night all of a sudden—and the next thing I knew, he peeled out of the driveway like an enraged teenager, leaving me standing there. I had a split second where I could not wear the damn mask anymore, a second where I just didn't want to fake it. This was what happened when he was out, God only knew where. I stopped thinking about how to fix it; I stopped pretending and asked my daughter if she was prepared to leave, and to leave a lot behind, again. She said yes fast, as she hates his guts. Any doubt I had about where we were sleeping that night immediately brought a picture of his whores to mind. The latest picture I had found on Facebook was one in which a woman was wearing his work jacket with his company logo, with the comment, "It's been a while…" It was the same damn jacket he gave to me!

Anger is a very powerful thing, and it gave me strength. I no longer had a single box in the house and decided we were leaving first thing in the morning. I could no longer ask for help, as no one in my family would speak to me. I piled and filled our closets with bags full of our stuff. I hid a few large bags behind the dresser where there was space. My attachment to my things was disappearing, and my need for safety was growing. It was a Friday. He worked almost every Saturday, but even if he didn't go to work, he left the house. I did not care—I was leaving anyway.

He eventually came home around 11 p.m., went to his room and shut the door. He never said a word to me. I felt no fear this time and went to bed. My feelings were frozen, on hold. When I woke up he was still in bed, obviously not rushing out of here for a change. The smell in his end of the house was suffocating, and I opened a window. I put my ear to his door—his fan was on high. I felt a chill run up my spine, but I was sticking to my plan. I was walking out, with him right in the house. I told my daughter to start loading the bags and dog into the car and to be quiet. We were done quickly, and I finally started shaking. I put my ear to his door again, urging myself to get out and not take any more stuff, the car was full. He was still asleep, locked in his room. I got into the car and felt the air change, the energy change all around me. I felt the future. I waited half an hour before texting him that we had left, that I would return the car to him later. He got me the car, put it in his company's name with me as the primary driver. He used it against me often, telling me he would tell the police I stole his car if I left, and I believed him.

I planned on going to community college and applying for financial aid, getting a job, as I was suddenly homeless and jobless. I told myself I could do it, start over again, work and go to school. He started calling the day I left. I ignored him for two whole weeks. I went to my ex's house and stayed in the basement. I didn't even really ask him. I really needed to be with my kids. Once, when he asked me how long I was staying and how I planned on supporting myself (I never asked him for a penny), I had the urge to leave. I was starting to feel overwhelmed, as I did not have a place to stay long term; and that very day, **he** came. My son heard it first. I was sitting on the couch, and he said, "Jay's here," like it was an everyday, normal occurrence. His car was loud outside, and I jumped up to go outside, as I did not want any drama here. I walked up to the passenger window. He rolled it down and said, "Get in."

I said, "No." For an hour or more, my feet aching from standing on the pavement in the street, I listened to him tell me how much he loved me, how sorry he was, that we could work it out, we were stronger together than apart, that he needed my help.

"Please help me with my problems. Help me. I love you," he said.

I told him to leave, and he finally did. The next two days were quiet; my kids, busy doing their own thing. There was no school as it was summer. By day three, the texts started again. This time, I responded. When I was out of the house I could tell him how I felt. He would never listen when we were together. He seemed to listen only when he was away from me. He said he understood how I felt and why I left, that he wanted me to be happy, that I had to give him back the car, that he would help me get a cheaper one. He said I could come get my stuff, that it was safe. I ignored what I knew deep inside. He stirred up the mental battle within me. I started to rationalize: My boys liked him, but they did not know him. I was a loser if I stayed in New Jersey. With Jay I had a life. My sons loved visiting PA. I could at least give them that.

* * *

THE NEXT DAY, I drove up with my oldest son in his truck. We planned on at least getting a mattress or two. Jay was at work, and he promised not to be there. My thoughts were crazy the whole way there: *I hate living in my ex's basement. I don't like the rat race in New Jersey. When did I fall in love with the Pennsylvania mountains, with the sky?* We pulled into his circular driveway an hour and a half later, and I almost fainted. He was sitting right there on the front steps. He was home waiting for me on a weekday, looking peaceful, but I knew better.

For more than two hours, we loaded nothing in the car; instead, we did something we had never done before: we talked. He did not allow me to load anything, despite my protests. He was pretending to be human, even crying. His apologies were loud and sincere; his declarations of how much he needed me, pulling me in and off my guard. My only desire, all of these years, should have been to leave him and never look back. But the truth is, what I wanted just a drop more was for him to be what he said he was, what he claimed to be in the beginning, what I needed him to be… but what he never will be.

My son started frantically texting me from the other side of the house: "Mom, please, give him another chance. Jay is part of our family." He kept going with how much he loved it there and that he was starving. I forgot that I brought him in part because I knew I would be safer with him; instead, I told him to join us outside, gave him some cash, and sent him to buy himself lunch. He said he would drive to his favorite pizza place twenty minutes away. I started to tell myself the same lies, that at least offering this to my children was something, that maybe it would ease my guilt a little bit pertaining to what they had lost in my divorce from their dad. All lies.

What happened next had happened before, but I still was not ready, didn't expect it, and couldn't stop it. He grabbed my hand and pulled me into the house. He talked very fast, telling me over and over how he missed and loved me, and not letting me get a word in. He then said we should call my mom and bring her and my daughter to pick out a ring that night. I was brave and told him what a piece of shit he was and asked him to please finally tell me the truth—did he sleep with Shantell? He looked me straight in the eyes, green eyes to green eyes, lied to my face and said, "No." I chose to believe him yet again.

* * *

I HAD WAITED two years for his apology, and I wanted a stable and normal life more than I wanted to be hurt and see the truth. I couldn't believe, not back then, that people could be so bad. I made a choice that day. I felt it shift, and I could not control it. I suddenly did not want to be alone with him. Things were moving so fast, but a little voice inside my head told me that this was what I had wanted all along, that he was telling the truth and that he loved me. He wouldn't say it if he didn't, right?!?!?!

* * *

HIS EYES WERE SUDDENLY BLAZING with lust. He pushed me against the kitchen counter and started kissing me—another shock—really kissing me, and not taking no for an answer. Why the hell couldn't I resist him, why? He kept going, telling me that I was a better person than him, as I pushed his hands off of me to no avail. He was strong; his large hands, cupping and squeezing my breasts; his tongue, darting around inside my mouth, making it hard to say anything at all. I felt my knees suddenly go weak, and he knew he had won, he had me. He dragged me into the bedroom and actually locked the door. I knew my verbal protests meant nothing to either of us as my body responded to him, also betraying me. He put his strong arms around me, closed his eyes, asked me to accept him for who he was, to love him, then pulled my pants down.

I told myself on the ride back to New Jersey, no furniture to be seen in the truck, that I really didn't want to start over, be away from my kids, because I would have to work two jobs to support myself and go back to school. I told myself that no one is perfect and that I could live with him, in that beautiful house, and even get married. I just forgot that I cannot survive without loyalty.

15

PLANNING TO ELOPE

My daughter willingly came back, as it was too crowded at her dad's house. Jay handed her money to go clothes shopping and bought the boys a quad that weekend. We also booked a trip for Vegas. He did it—two first class tickets and a wedding ceremony at Planet Hollywood Chapel for New Year's Eve. Everyone admired my gorgeous two-carat ring that my mom and daughter helped me pick out. We had decided to elope, telling only our immediate families. This is another thing that I let go of. I wanted our families' support, wanted them to be a part of it, but he wouldn't budge, so I agreed.

He kept joking with the kids: "Now that your mother is staying, let's put in a pool," and other things, leading them to believe it was all my fault and he was so innocent. I let it all go; I was free to do what I wanted. I was working part time from home, I had no financial stress, and gas in my car. I could see my sons whenever I wanted to. He seemed happy, like he had what he wanted. Things looked different with a ring on my finger. I loved the house, the huge yard, the long windows that let in so much light. I made a mental list of things to do to make it feel cozier, like home.

* * *

WE ARE GETTING MARRIED in twelve weeks. It is odd to plan a wedding that needs no planning, not to have any friends or family attending. My sisters still aren't speaking to me. My daughter is doing dance and piano now, and I tell myself this is normal, and normal is good, as I listen to her giggle on the phone with her friends. I dropped her off at dance tonight and went home to get his dinner ready. It was on the table when he walked in. He ate it, made a second plate, then had some cookies. He immediately got on his phone and also his iPad. We had an hour alone, and the whole time he stared at a computer screen. I tell myself he is exhausted from work, stressed and tired, but keep thinking he will look at me, see me, touch me. I wonder if I have become needy, if I am addicted to his rejection, if he is even rejecting me. I remind myself how much he has done for me, for us, in just a few short weeks. I ignore the screaming voice inside of me that says, *Don't marry him.* He offers to go with me to pick up my daughter; he gets in the passenger side and falls asleep.

During the next few weeks, I am feeling so empty again, scared even. He is not at all affectionate, not loving, not kind, and not even sexual. I feel stifled, trapped, hungry, tricked. He sends me a text the next day, "I had an amazing weekend with you and the kids. You make me so happy." He spells out the words, "I love you." I tell myself to adjust, be strong, believe him, go against all of my instincts, buy lottery tickets.

The weeks fly by, and I feel the water rising around my neck. I have a life jacket on, but it is not strapped, does not fit. I start to pack for Vegas, throwing my cheap wedding dress in a suitcase. As the days and weeks fly by, I see my kids doing well and keep my mouth shut. We have tickets to go to several shows including Britney Spears. When we get back, we will be married. We are having a few family members, the ones still speaking to me, over to celebrate after we return. I feel the hole getting bigger with all of the people that will be missing.

I continue to placate him, tend to him and his needs, ignore my own. I clean the house and try to avoid stress in all forms. I stop myself from telling him to slow down on the rare occasions that he does drive; it is always a terrifying experience. He thinks he is skilled, his ego massive, but he is very reckless. I remind myself how I wanted normalcy, sameness, while simultaneously craving a way out. Moving no longer feels like an option, as I watch my daughter spreading her wings. I won't fail her, not today.

I am living in some sort of fog. I honestly don't really know if either one of us will go through with the ceremony. I cannot picture it. Tomorrow we leave for Vegas.

16

VEGAS

We left for the airport, got through security quickly, and were seated in our first-class seats. He made calls before takeoff, and I took pictures. He told me he was wearing a custom-made Evil Knievel® suit, and I just shook my head at him. He was obsessed with himself and how he looked, like he was trying to impress an invisible fan club. He never once asked me what I was wearing.

The first night, we saw Britney, which I loved. I knew every word and had a blast dancing with the two gay guys seated next to me. Jay sat in his seat during the entire show. He couldn't even see her from where he sat.

The weather was beautiful for December, and we walked everywhere and went sightseeing and saw a magic show on the second night, from front row seats. All I could think about was the fact that this was our honeymoon, night two of four, and he hadn't touched me yet. By the fourth and last night, the night we were getting married, I figured he was saving it for after. I took out my cheap dress, put on my sexy underwear, and did a great job with my makeup. He kept asking me how *he* looked. We were about to go have a drink at the bar before the ceremony when he grabbed me and pushed me roughly onto the bed. It was uneventful and a little heartbreaking. On the way down to the bar, he kept looking at himself in all of the mirrors. We were getting married in an hour. We sat at the bar, and he actually talked to the young woman on his right the whole time, so I chatted with the woman on my left. We walked over to the chapel and said our vows, and it was done. He dipped me and kissed me and then picked me up and put me over his shoulder, which made for some great pictures. I felt disconnected the rest of the night. We went to our room to watch fireworks from the window and went to sleep. *You heard me.*

    I kept waiting for something to be different, to be better, for us to be closer. It seemed to mean nothing to him, his first time ever getting married, and it seemed to not have even happened.

17

EIGHTEEN DAYS LATER

*P*ain. I watch a Christmas ornament roll across the street under a car. It jingles as it rolls, seems to be in slow motion, its colors swirling around in endless circles. My son made this beautiful ornament. I am so tired, but I force myself to go and get it. I force one foot in front of the other…it is important that I have my things. I take whatever will fit inside the car. We had another fight, he got violent, I ran. I run around the house, trying to decide what is important to me now, so sure this time that I will never be back. My things, again, in garbage bags, pillowcases, suitcases. My daughter and my dog try to see over the seat in the overstuffed car. Leaving my stuff leaves a bigger hole in me this time. Eighteen days married and this, again. My antique hutch, my wine glasses, Starbucks mugs, my pictures, each frame picked with loving care, the photos of my family, smiling inside them.

I am at my sister's this time, forty minutes away. I feel the tension in me tighten, its grip never really loosening. I need a plan. I need to focus. Why does this have to hurt so much? Everything hurts. I feel judged, homeless, stupid, as my life spins in a dryer with the door wide open. I am so sick of this, of being put in the same position, but I had no choice but to leave. It feels like I am choosing life when I leave. Then the immediate crash comes. I tell myself I don't have the energy for this. I am afraid and angry all at once. I feel like a loser. No one could ever possibly understand; I know that now. No one could ever understand the monster.

"Hi!" my sister says and comes outside as she sees us pull up, her thick, curly, auburn hair blowing in the wind. I notice her make-up, her pretty, casual dress, her funky bracelets. I see her porch swing, the cozy rocking chairs, the random angels she has placed near the lush, healthy plants.

"Hi," I say. I tell her thanks for letting us stay and that we will only be there a few days. I am aware how awkward it is to see her, to ask for help, but I am in crisis mode. She is not judging me, just opening her door.

It is imperative for my own sanity that I remain calm. I know that she sees through my calm. My dog barks and I want to sink to the ground, maybe take a nap, but I balance the ornament, my wrist stinging from the leash my dog pulls. I look over at my daughter, my baby girl, and she is smiling, running over to her cousin, who is six months younger than her. My Cali, 12 going on 20, has seen way too much drama, her long, blonde hair, blue-green eyes, her brilliance even surpassing her beauty. Her fearless support of me and her flawless ability to adapt has made me respect and admire her at such a young age. "Mom, he is such a jerk to you—let's go!" We both miss being free of him, being able to shut the door at the end of the day and sing karaoke.

* * *

WE HAD ANOTHER FIGHT, MY "HUSBAND" and I. It was brutal this time; he got physical, crazy. I was too tired to pretend to be happy anymore. I honestly didn't know I was in an abusive relationship and developing depression. The truth is I married a zombie—he is sick and evil. I tried to keep his secret, but I cannot sleep, I cannot eat, I am afraid. I repeat to myself, over and over, the last words he said to me, three nights ago, horrible words, too horrible to share. The worst words you can even think of. More disturbing than his dirty mouth was the look on his face. He growled at me like a rabid animal, grinding his teeth, spitting out his smut toward me, which reminded me why I stayed silent, didn't provoke him. I asked for a divorce after the fight, asked to keep it amicable, like two adults. I told him we tried, getting married and all, we really tried. He then took my keys, my car, my freedom. I sat in the house for two days and decided to lie to his face instead, let him actually touch me, accept his apology. When he finally believed everything was okay, then I left.

As I drove, I remembered how we met, this man I married. He was 6'2," muscular, had straight brown hair and kept it short. He had green eyes, large hands, a deep, sexy voice and, later I learned, a vile temper. I remembered his profile picture, our first date, or second, when he brought me to his empty house. I was following him in my car, this man I met on a dating website. He wanted to show me his house. He took a slow spin around the circular driveway, and I wondered if he was too old to be living with his parents. He led me down the back driveway to the back of the house where double garage doors made of glass stood. Once inside, I appreciated the granite countertops, the ceramic tiles in earth tones. I also noticed the echo, the emptiness, no parents, and no knick-knacks either. There was much beauty but no warmth to be felt; it was odd and confusing, like him. There was a couch, a staircase, a bed in the bedroom but no pictures on the wall, no personal items anywhere. *Did he actually even live here,* I wondered. "Wow, this is beautiful. How long have you lived here?" I asked, expecting him to say a year or less, but he said eight—it all seemed so strange. I was kind of sad for him.

* * *

THE SOUND of my sister's dog barking wakes me from the too small bed in the too small room that is my niece's. I try to act normal but feel myself pull inwards even more, if this is even possible. What am I doing here, imposing on my sister and her family, when we haven't even spoken for months? I feel suddenly so old, humiliated, disrespected, unloved. My sister and her husband are being nothing but kind and generous, but so much damage was done. I see the farce of my life I worked so hard to hide becoming exposed, and I just don't want the invasion of privacy.

Not two days later, I wake up at "home." He comes for me, for my stuff, talks me out of leaving. I go with him. My daughter, needing her space, is ready, comes willingly.

18

THIS ISN'T LOVE

I wake up, not sure where I am for a second, which house I am in. I try my best to sleep, but I am so hot, I roll from side to side, adjusting my pillows and blankets, praying for comfort. My dog leaves; he can't sleep either because of me. I hear his feet coming down the hall. Something in me freezes. I lay perfectly still and hope he goes into the bathroom, or dies. He walks into my bedroom and says my name loudly, as if I were anywhere but in my bed. "Mirandaaaaaaa?" Come here.

"Yes," I say and roll over to look at him. He reaches out for my arm and, without me moving an inch, pulls it up and onto his body. I realize he has locked my door. I try to say I am tired, but he always gets what he wants. He takes what he wants. He sees nothing else. He appears to be trying in some way. I try not to scream or run or laugh. He is actually trying to kiss me now, trying to see me or make me see him, but I no longer care. In the back of my mind, I wonder, in a fleeting thought, if his teenaged girlfriend just dumped him or something. He cannot see me now —it is too late. I know what is inside of him, that the monster is there. In order to protect myself now, I control all of my emotions, all of the time. He never puts his arms around me, never rubs my neck or shoulders, never touches my hair…*How could I not have noticed this before?* He puts a hand on my hip but just to hold me where he needs me to be, and he takes what he wants. It feels good. I have completely lost myself to survive.

19

PAIN

It had to rain on me a million times
For me to see it,
The poison, bitter hate and betrayal in it.
It had to rain and rain and rain
For it to fill me,
To fill my eyes and drain,
For them to sting and burn and lie
And hurt so hard and sharp for me to feel it.
It had to pour and rain and rip the trees
And tear my heart out and make me bleed
So I believed it…

Written by: Melissa Sachs

OH TRUST, you bastard. The level of trust that was ripped from me still sends shock waves into my life, my soul, my dreams, my day. I cannot, will not, ever trust him again. I actually tried, but it is impossible as he is not sorry. The more I looked the more I saw:

inappropriate texts between him and his now married ex, strange emails to Russian women he had taken away for the weekend while we were fighting. Any kind of loyalty did not exist. I feel so stupid, and worse than the devastating and torturous visions of him with other women that haunt me are the lies. The lies haunt me worse because now when he speaks it seems like he is lying. I am now that woman who is always wondering where he really is, and for this I will not forgive him. I always think I see his car where it shouldn't be, always assume he is dirty with the sweat and sex of someone else on him. He does not deserve for me to feel this way, be in pain over him, but I cannot stop it and have learned to allow myself my feelings. I am too moralistic to "get even" but I believe my time will come, and karma is a bitch. My "husband," the abusive, lying, cheating asshole with no feelings or conscience or soul, will get what he deserves.

 Today is Friday, and the monster came home early. He asked me if I checked the movie times without even saying hello. He did not even look at me, his mind on food as usual. We usually see a movie and go to dinner on Fridays, which is the extent of our social lives. We have no friends, no parties, nothing to look forward to. Somewhere inside, I am still me, I think. I used to have tons of friends, from my children's school, from the gym I taught classes at, from my neighborhood. I used to host parties and events and holidays right on my front lawn, not even be able to go to the supermarket without running into two or three people I knew. I am stuck here with the monster and the realization that I am not able to actually build a life with him, have a life with him. If you look at me you won't see it, my brokenness. I look healthy, but I stopped smiling a while ago. People look at me and assume that I actually have what they want. I am truly alone.

 At the movie, he doesn't actually lick his fingers after eating the largest bucket of popcorn they sell; he sucks each one slowly, putting the whole thing in his mouth. I tell myself even his mouth and stomach are sick, out of control. The monster is an evil, full of rage and illness, that lives inside of him; it is always there and can come out at any given time. It has never tried to hide, never tried to blend in, or be less. He is an antisocial beast and makes no apologies. I hate him today, more than usual. I hate how my life has become so diminished and he is thriving. I don't want to wear this hat anymore. I ache for my freedom. I see my daughter happy, try to make the best of it, then mourn my life. It is a nightmare out of hell.

* * *

MY MIND TAKES me back to my mistakes, to the beginning, back to the beautiful house I bought when I first moved here. A Victorian, over 100 years old, beautiful beyond words, and near my family. The front porch is wide, with a swing on the right. There are three staircases with beautiful, decorative wood railings. The molding stands out in every room along with the arched doorways. The kitchen is small but cozy with a huge window. It is perfect.

I have so much furniture that I need nothing; anything that I added from the local antique "shoppes" is pure, delicious icing. I take great pleasure in filling my home with the things that I love for my family, shutting us inside at the end of the day. The landing on the second floor is a dream, large enough for a seating area; the narrow back stairs leading to the kitchen are even beautiful. I hang pictures of the kids up and down the walls. The house feels like Christmas to me.

* * *

THAT MAY HAVE BEEN my only chance to own my own home; I pray that is not true. If I ever get the chance again I will cherish every second of it. I will sing and dance throughout each room; I will cook and clean and just be me again.

When I sold my house, I had a garage sale, most of my stuff going to my own family as I did not need all of it. I had so much, and it did not really match his house. Now when I go to my grandmother's, my sister's, I see my own stuff staring at me, my own past that I long for, cry for, lovingly displayed in their homes. They have no idea I feel this way; taking my stuff that day only helped me declutter and move. *That candleholder was mine,* I think, *that light, the washer and dryer.* Each item has a story unbeknownst to them, lost to me, forever.

There are too many things to count, cutting boards and blankets…I want them back, along with my house and my soul.

20

THE PARTY

He came into my room this morning, took off his clothes and lay down on my bed. He put one finger in the edge of my underwear, not to touch me, just to slide them down, while lying on his back. He pulled me on top of him, making sure I felt his readiness, proud to show it off. My legs straddling him, my urge to fight feeling lost, my disappointment at never having my own needs met put on hold, the illusion of temporary warmth and human contact pulling me in. *This is not love,* I tell myself; it never was. His shoulders are sculpted, so strong. I fit so perfectly into him, every angle. I am unable to forget how cold he is inside while he satisfies his own need and acts like he did some magnificent favor for me. Later, I get a text telling me that I am hot and that he loves me.

I jump in the shower then on the treadmill that he bought me and walk fast to try to outpace my thoughts, while watching *Dexter* on Netflix®. Being here alone is pure bliss. He invades every inch of my space when he is here, changes every particle of energy in any room he enters. After a few hours on the computer, I go to get my coffee at the local Starbucks. The people at the drive-through window are so nice; they laugh and interact and smile, and I see a glimpse, almost a memory or vision of happier times, reminding me they could be in my future. I remember that I was like them before, light-hearted and happy, and that my life does not have to stay this way—I can be happy again.

We are celebrating my daughter's thirteenth birthday tonight. She invited eight of her friends and classmates to come over. They are painting pumpkins and having pizza and cake. Most of the girls took the bus home with her, leaving shoes, coats and backpacks all over the foyer. I try not to think of the fight I had with Jay today, hoping he just won't come home at all.

We were never "friends" on Facebook. He refused, which should have told me something. He claimed it was a temporary page he needed for an upcoming class reunion, that he hated Facebook and would be deleting it after the reunion.

After cleaning the entire house, planning all the details for the birthday party, running alone, working out, and taking a shower, I still had time on my hands. What can I say? I am very organized. I decided to pull a high school move with the goal being to quiet the doubt inside me.

* * *

I HAD NEVER in my life done this before, ever, but I looked him up. I did not expect to find anything, though I admit my entire body was shaking. His Facebook was on private, but I was able to see his friends list. *Who were these people*, I wondered, *all of his local high school friends I have never seen or met, still living close by?* When the young slut Shantell popped up my heart rate tripled. I could not believe he was friends with her, and I kept telling myself I was not seeing her tiny picture there in a yellow nightgown.

The picture of the very girl who haunts my days and nights was standing in this very kitchen, as if I would not recognize it. I went into a kind of tailspin then, my brain trying to explain to my heart it wasn't true. There must be some sort of explanation. With my daughter and her friends about to be home, I prayed for balance but could not find it. I could not fake being okay right now; I could barely breathe. So I called him.

For a change, I acted without thought. I needed him to help me understand so I could process, so I could function. He answered and I simply demanded an explanation. Once I started yelling I could not stop, because you have to believe what is right in front of you at some point. What had I gotten myself into, moving my child, changing her school, selling my home, giving up lifetime alimony, marrying this lying bastard?

Who the hell is he? He told me he was in a meeting and actually hung up the phone. As infuriated and as right as I was, I was also terrified. I felt him coming. I knew he was walking out of that meeting and on his way. I was really afraid, I won't lie. I swear that piece of shit marched into the kitchen, roughly pulled me into his bedroom and started screaming and yelling at ME!

"I was in a meeting with my dad," he roared, his lips twitching and stretched over his growling teeth. "I must have forgotten to delete her. Facebook is stupid; why would you spend your time on there?" he yelled at the top of his lungs. His yelling literally backed me up all the way to the farthest wall in his room, which was his bathroom where I sat down on the closed toilet. I was not yet ready to back down, because maybe he thinks Facebook is stupid but I am not. I was about to tell him to take his lies and go die in a hole when I saw the switch, the sudden change in him, similar to what a great white must look like as it is about to take a bite of another living thing, its eyes rolling back in its head. The rage I had released quickly woke me up and made me remember who I was dealing with, and I shut my mouth. It was too late, though. Sitting on the toilet with him half over me, with nowhere to go, knowing he had lost control, I tried to become as small as possible. He lifted up his size 13 work boot and proceeded to kick the shower wall in half, his boot barely missing my face. He kicked it over and over, even when it was down, and I got on my hands and knees and crept out of the room, realizing again he was crazy, he could kill me. He walked by me, making growling noises, slammed the door and went back to work.

* * *

THAT WAS SEVERAL HOURS AGO. The party is now well underway, the girls not needing me at all. I heat up pizzas as they chat, dance, and paint. I hold the rage inside of me. I am thinking he is to blame for me standing here all alone, when he suddenly walks in. He walks right by me, straight to his bedroom, and shuts the door.

I remember so many of my kids' birthday parties when my own family and friends would attend, celebrate with me, keep me company, make memories. My hate for him is growing by the second. I no longer care what he will do. The party will be over and he will have ruined this, too, for me. He eventually comes out of his room, like a bear with messed up hair, smelling food. He glares at me, and for the second time that day, I feel stupidly brave. I glare back, unafraid to ask him, "Do you hear that?" the girls' laughter getting louder and louder.

He answers "Yes."

And I say, "Good, because you will never hear it again," and I turn my back on him, feeling stupidly protected with the kids in the next room, until I feel his hand on me, pulling me in the opposite direction into the dining room. He looks crazy as he calls me a fucking bitch. He grabs my wrist and tries to take my ring off my finger. My hand and wrist instantly hurt. I told him to please stop, that I would give him the ring. I defiantly take off my gorgeous, two-carat, white-gold, diamond ring and throw it across the room while looking him in the eye. The shock and horror on his face almost makes me run, but I cannot because my child is here.

* * *

I STORMED AWAY, back to check on the kids, who were fine. They had food and were talking about boys like the world was perfect. I had used his half-empty garage showroom and had the glass garage doors open, as it was a beautiful day. He was behind me, using two hands to guide me roughly outside. He pulled me down a rock wall toward the back of the house, where I had to jump about three feet down with him holding me, or my arm would have detached from my body. He then threw me against the back of the house and put his hands around my neck. I was out of breath, my back against the house, with a crazy person's hands around my neck, who was twice my size. Oh, he was here alright —the monster out in full force! I was in self-preservation mode then and wondered who was speaking out of my mouth, begging him to let me go, not to hurt me and that I was sorry. I felt his hands on my collar bones as I continued pleading with him to stop. He somehow never left a mark on my body other than a temporary red mark here and there. I kept lying telling him how stressed and alone I felt. I needed him; this was my daughter's party, very important to me. He let go and went back into his cave, leaving me standing there, suddenly cold.

I climbed the rocks, smiled at the girls, and died inside. I hoped my neck wasn't too red and heard the doorbell ring. The girls were suddenly starting to get picked up, and I endured compliments about the house and tried not to break down to total strangers and beg for them to get me out of there. I felt like another species compared to the parents that came and went. The two kids staying the night with my daughter were already upstairs whispering and giggling, wrapped in their sleeping bags. I did some light cleaning, told myself that my daughter had a blast, and crawled into bed. I felt weary, tired beyond words. I blinked and it was morning.

* * *

I SLEEP like a champion for a change, and I rub my dog's back and get a stunned chill as he steps into my room. He gets into my bed, and I hop up like an Olympic athlete and am on my feet, as I would rather die than lie next to him right now. He softly says my name, and I look over to see tears streaming down his face. I did not know monsters could cry. He must not see the ice coming off me as he starts with his apologies, telling me how he loves me and that his medication must be off again. This time he adds that he cannot live without me.

I hear feet upstairs and won't fight in front of my child. He is still talking, "You just make me so mad sometimes," he says. I am too upset to fight; I know what I will get. I know I have to plan, stay in control, keep my daughter safe.

I tell him I am going to make pancakes for my daughter and her friends and leave the room. He follows me and actually tells jokes that make the kids laugh at breakfast. When they are done, they go outside to run with the dog. I start cleaning the dishes when I feel him behind me; I turn and see the look in his eye. He tells me we should take a walk around the lake later, spend time together, and he pushes me against the sink and tries to kiss me, a real kiss. I push him away then betray myself and kiss him back, whoever he is. He takes my hand and slips the ring inside my palm.

I put it on.

CONCLUSION

There are really no words to describe how this experience has impacted me, my life, my future, my children. My self-esteem took the hit of the century. My growth did as well. I am now in total control of myself; any temper that I ever had is gone due to having to survive for so many years by keeping him calm. This is a gift, and really all we have in life. Self-control.

I currently live a few miles from the monster. Am I totally free? Not yet, although I am divorced, and he is not the father of my children. He is still a terrifying thing, and I am always on guard. I jump when a loud car goes by or my dog barks. My daughter did, too, until just recently. I carry guilt for having exposed her to this. My sons are older and still think he is cool and want to be like the parts of him they see and admire. For example, he is a car dealer and collector, and that is every boy's dream, right?

The worst part of this is he still talks to my children, and I have to deal with this as they are over 18 and I was the one who tried for years to get them to like him. They never saw him throw me against the wall or choke me or try to break my wrist or run me off the road or rape me. They never saw me on the floor or crying and debating driving into the woods or sitting in front of the hospital and almost going in a dozen times but waiting out the pain and heading "home" instead. They never saw their sister calling 911 or hiding in her room or begging me to leave again or telling me she is scared. I have to live with all of this.

My daughter is the epitome of strength, and I pray she makes better decisions than I ever did. My sons, smart beyond words, incredibly beautiful, talented young men—they will see the truth in time. I will give them that time. I can tell you that my children have two parents who could not love them more.

As far as my future goes, it is finally bright. I locked myself in my room for almost a year to fight this depression that will be with me forever, and I recently decided to come out and do more than force myself to go to the supermarket. I decided to go out on a date. I have been seeing this new man for three months, keeping him at a distance that is comfortable for me. I can tell you that this one isn't a narcissist. I know very well what to look for!

I chose him not only because of his incredible capacity to give endless amounts of love but also because of his ability to receive it. I know what it feels like to love someone with all that you have, with all that you are, and to not get it in return. I know the hollow death of a soul. I traveled through a dark tunnel and came out alive. I also know the pain and guilt associated with a good man loving you with all he has and the inability to naturally give him the same in return, simply because you cannot match his feelings.

The fearless ability to safely love a man cannot be downplayed. The risk is immense and infinite, and even when returned, the imminent thoughts that one of you will someday leave, even if it is not until death, lies awake at the back of your mind.

But this very privilege is what it is to LIVE. And live I will. I am not able to love as much as him, this new man in my life. I am too afraid it will consume all of me and there will be nothing left, and I have children to put ahead of me; **I cannot be nothing**.

ADDENDUM: FINDING LIKE SURVIVORS SAVED MY LIFE

The first amazing six months turned into seven years of actual hell. I lost everything to a lying, cheating monster. The physical abuse was nothing compared to what he did to my soul, my spirit, my confidence, my finances, and my relationships with my children. My entire life has changed because I did not listen to myself or see the flags.

I still work every day to control my thoughts, to not be hurt by him, to heal. I still allow myself to feel the pain but would never let him see, never let him in, never repeat my mistake. I, sadly, may never trust again, but this feels right to me, safe.

Fighting and revenge, in my opinion and experience, is too dangerous. Fight with the devil? No thanks! I have given him enough of my time, been used enough. I liked myself much better before; my innocent, trusting attitude was everything. I believed that nothing could hurt me. But that person is dead now. My new self, the one who did not die—she is strong and sad, a fighter and broken, alive and sometimes afraid. I will put her together and nurture and protect her, put her first, along with my children, the way I always should have from the beginning. I will forgive her and end the criticism in her head, because there is much more. Life is just beginning for me, at 47 years old, and I am grateful.

Please, PLEASE, don't give up. You are not alone. Email me for help and advice: narccanthaveme@gmail.com

WHAT TO LOOK FOR TO AVOID A NARCISSISTIC, ABUSIVE RELATIONSHIP:

I am a survivor of domestic abuse, entailing physical, emotional, and sexual abuse. It started verbally and ended violently. The worst part for me is the psychological damage that was left inside of me.

FIRST OF ALL, **what is abuse?**
Anything that is unhealthy for you as far as the way someone treats you. The abuser could be your mother, your father, your boss, your boyfriend, lover, or husband.

TOO MUCH TOO SOON:
After just having met someone, even a few weeks or months in, you still don't really know him. There is no shortcut to this process.
Watch out for these signs:
He...

- ...is being unbelievably LOVING.

- …is totally ATTENTIVE.
- …is crazy GENEROUS (with his time, emotions, money).
- …always AGREES with you on everything.
- …is the perfect SEXUAL partner you have always dreamed of.

Any or all of these should scream **something isn't right**! He is watching you, he is mimicking you, and he is not genuine. What is he is hiding?

WHY WOULD he like what you like all of the time? Why would your hobbies, your dreams, be his? Why is a stranger even helping you to achieve your goals? For **control**—that is his ultimate goal, **his power over you**. Why would he be a clone of you? Were you not interested in finding someone who understands you, who appreciates you, who compliments and supports you? You were not ever interested in a clone or a zombie with no feelings or hobbies or dreams of his own, were you?

WHAT IT FEELS LIKE:

Well, amazing!!! You finally found the love of your life, a compatible partner in all ways—the way you think, dream, feel, love, act. The support and joy are overwhelming. Your sense of self becomes stronger. You feel fulfilled and believe that you were right all along. You were waiting for this person; you feel like you found your soul mate. You feel like you are in love, and that clouds your judgement. That binds you to him in your mind.

WHAT IT LOOKS LIKE:

Other people in your life simply see you happy. And even

though, later, some will tell you they saw flags or never liked him, they trust *you* and they are living their own lives, so they are happy for you. They are often jealous; they want what you have.

I had one girl that I really liked, one of my only new friends I made after moving to Pennsylvania, tell me she would not be at our engagement party because she did not like him. She had a funny feeling around him, and she did not like the way he looked at me or how quiet he was when other people were with us. I never spoke to her again, already having put him first in all ways. I was very upset and hurt by what she said. I now think this girl had some experience, some bad experience with a narcissist or someone, even a parent, who abused her in some way and she was trying to warn me.

What is Actually Happening:

I had heard the word "narcissist," of course, although I had no clue what it really meant in its true form; but the terms "love-bombing" and "trauma bond" were foreign to me.

Do you actually think someone exists who is your twin? A person out there who intrinsically understands or "gets" every single thing about you? Your entire thought process, your goals the way you dream, the way you parent, your hobbies? A person who will blindly accept you on all levels and show love and support? **Well, I can tell you the answer is no.** Love-bombing is just that: it is an empty, evil, soulless monster mimicking your every amazing move, your feelings. Listen, listen harder—**They have no feelings**. They are unable to feel or to connect to anyone in a genuine way, yet they crave this and are jealous of it, of you. The way they get their fuel to live, to feed their enormous egos is to eat good people's emotions, over and over and over, until some of us are drained of all life, until some of us give up, until some of us die. Don't let them take you.

This all happens very quickly; you don't have a chance to look up, to evaluate, to think. What is serious stalking you see as him wanting you; what is overwhelming amounts of time together is actually him starting to control you and what you do and where you go and who you see and where you work and who you talk to and even how you think. **They actually study you.** This is a terrifying concept, as they use all they learn against you in some twisted way later.

Even during the first few weeks that I met him, I felt love. But when I look back at our first night together, after too many drinks at my house and me ending up very sick in the bathroom, he still pulled me into my bedroom. He then took what he wanted, against my verbal protests. There is a word for that, my first experience with him, the first time he took without permission and then romanticized it; and I accepted this, blamed myself for drinking. The word is rape! **He...raped...me!** And I stayed. The whole thing was very confusing because I could never match his actions to his words, and this was new territory to me. I had no idea what I was dealing with.

He was a liar his whole life and a criminal with no respect for authority. **Flag!** He had no fear of getting in trouble, ever, no fear of police officers, of jail, of lying, of consequences. I care nothing for how his father abused him and his current, horrific trauma bond with this man, not anymore. As adults we have to stop blaming our parents for everything; we have to seek answers and growth and healing and take responsibility for our own lives and our own choices.

He was lying and cheating on me from the beginning. The amount of attention he showed me left me in a state. I only realized later he was doing the same to other women (narcissistic supply), some of them half my age. When this happens to you it isn't like you think. You don't just say "screw this," and walk away. You are baffled beyond belief. You cannot see through the fog of their words verses their actions; it is impossible because of the confusion they instill in you. I was devastated. It did not matter that he was a horrible person, that I did not want that in my life. I was in a state of shock. I was damaged to my core that someone could fool me so badly, someone I gave my whole self to, someone I thought I loved. It was October, 2009, when we met. He brought my whole family gifts for Christmas just eight weeks later. My sisters, my mother, my grandmother, my kids—they all thought he was the greatest thing that ever happened to me, at least for a minute anyway. This was a major **flag**! He was manipulating my family so that later, when I finally caught on, they would not believe me.

When the monster's mask slips—and it will, often— it is usually early on. I remember him being condescending to me on the phone, being very short. I remember being kind of in shock. I did not know rage; I did not know the signs; I did not know this person. The **apology** always came soon after, followed by the **excuse**. **Flags!** It took me *years* to see this pattern, despite the number of apologies on my phone at any given time, *years*. For example: he would call me and I would start to talk. He would get annoyed at any little thing and suddenly seem very short with me, then he would hang up on me. Later, he would call back and apologize, telling me some sob story about how hard his job was and how mean his dad was. I would actually end up *apologizing to him* (pattern) and listening to him. He always said how he needed help and he needed support. He made me feel bad every time, as if I was causing the problem. **Huge flag!**

WHAT IS ACTUALLY GOING ON:

He is using a system of **punishment and reward** (pattern), and you are in a total state of confusion. He is doing this on purpose. He has done this before. Read that again, please. **He has done this before.** He is good at this and will never stop. You will be replaced, and then she will be the next victim.

The perfect guy, the happiest you have ever been—that is who you still believe he is, even as his mask slips. You have no idea what is happening. It starts to feel like your world is ending when you fight (trauma bond). Then he comes back for you, and he will, over and over again. *You are the one to make excuses for him*—to your friends, to your family, but sadly, mostly to yourself. You think he is who you met, but he is not—he never was. He is no one. He is a fraud. He is a bully. He is a monster. You are literally incapable of understanding his game. Meanwhile, he is lying and cheating on you, and you are ignoring every single flag because you are becoming depressed.

You feel trapped—once again, the trauma bond.

TRAUMA BONDS, as explained by Shari Stines, Psy.D:

"You seem unable to detach from someone even though you cannot trust them and you do not like them."

"When you try to leave this person, you find yourself missing them to the point of LONGING that is so awful that you believe it is going to destroy you."

"Usually trauma bonds occur in relationships involving INCONSISTENT REINFORCMENT, such as those with addicts and alcoholics or in domestic violence situations. "

What Others See:

Drama! You suddenly lose your entire support system, including yourself—your judgement is gone. By fighting with him and asking for help, over and over, and returning to him, your friends and family start to blame you. After all, aren't you smart and giving and experienced? Are you not a reasonable grown-up, a parent? He is so calm, and you, well...you are a mess.

This was the plan. **He has done this before.**

Many times, over the six years I was with this person, I turned to him, to communicate, to help me understand, to tell him he needed to help me. I wanted to understand his behavior. I even wanted to be supportive despite the cheating and abuse. I always chose peace, which actually enraged him even more. *He wanted me off kilter; he wanted me broken; he wanted me dead.* He usually laughed in my face and blamed me after I tried to converse with him or to solve problems with him, and then he stayed out all night. By that point, I needed professional help, which I never got. It is a miracle I am still here. I believed, until the last two years, that he loved me. I was very wrong.

IMPACT ON HEALTH:

Depression is terrifying. It sucks you in as you scream to get out, and unless there are others like you, no one gets it. The most terrifying part is no one can save you now but **you**.

If you meet someone in this situation, you must help, as many times as needed, without judgement, for your words may be what saves them. You won't be able to tell who needs you; just be there for everyone you care about.

PATTERNS AND HOW YOU FEEL:

- Stop when you first meet someone, just stop. If things are moving too quickly, then something is wrong.
- Listen and feel. What are you feeling?
- Joy, pain, confusion, elation. This is not normal, not healthy. There should be more balance. Look closely at his behavior, without him knowing.
- His life is not genuine. Look at his friendships—he has none.
- Apologies: constant and plenty
- Rage: This is not normal or healthy. One should strive for self-control. He lost it with everyone, for no

reason. He loved to frighten everyone. It gave him power.
- Disrespect: Look at how he treats you in private, in public, and look at how you feel. Does he listen to you? Does he respond genuinely? Does he respect your boundaries? Make sure you define, to yourself, your boundaries, on every level—sexually, too—and see if he respects you.
- Isolation: Does he have good friends? Quality relationships at work? Is he keeping you from friends and family? I quit my job, sold my business, sold my house, changed my car, all because of him. *That is insane.*
- Greed: Is he kind? Is he giving? He was a criminal. He pitted his own employees against each other. He stole; he lied on taxes, to unemployment, to his family, to car dealers, to lawyers and judges, to the state, to everyone. To me.
- Abuse: It still stuns me that I was in an abusive relationship. It stuns me that I had opinions about these things, yet I was so wrong. I wish I didn't know. I wish I'd never met him, but I know. It isn't what you think: she can't "just leave." Trust me.
- Being afraid: I had never been afraid of a man before him. He was terrifying. He had no conscience, no connections, no remorse, no guilt. At first, I wished I could be like him. I had to allow myself to go through the pain of losing, and losing hard, and not let anger eat me alive. I was angry at an aggressive, narcissistic psychopath, so I had nowhere to put the anger.

BEING AFRAID ISN'T NORMAL, do you hear me? Placating someone isn't healthy, it isn't genuine—you lose who you are. You end up trying your best to get through, to figure it out, and years go by. **Losing who I was devastated me! He lost nothing; I lost everything.**

How to Get Out:

Run!

Find help outside of family, find other survivors, find groups, use hotlines. I'll say it again: **Find help outside of family!** Other survivors give you **validation,** and that saves you.

You have been in an abusive relationship, do you hear me? I was physically, emotionally, spiritually, and sexually assaulted, repeatedly, until I stopped it. I educated myself, and I got out. 911, judges, lawyers, parents—no one could help me against this evil, until I was ready. No one I knew understood. I was terrified of the man I married.

Sexually:

I thought he was so hot, so dominant, but the hair pulling and the taking and the public displays were all so abusive. Then the no sex at all the last *five years* was abuse, too. It was all so confusing. When you think someone loves you, the things you may allow him to do are astounding. When you find out he does them with others, your heart breaks in half, regardless of whether he is a bad person or not.

Our last encounter before I moved out, the day after our divorce was final, ended the same way it all began. I had too much to drink in celebrating my freedom (I literally only drank about once a year). After being dropped off at the house, I was in the bathroom, when he came in and followed me around until I was half passed out, not moving, and then he raped me. He did not hurt me physically, but I said "**No.**" I did not move or participate in any way, but that did not stop him. He is a disgusting, evil pig, and he rapes and lies and cheats and abuses women and children.

What a Day is Like with a Narcissist:
Everything is about their needs. They won't commit to anything but expect you to be available 24/7, regardless of whether you have children or animals or other plans. He used to park the car in a parking lot and sit for an hour. Although I had a young daughter to get home to, he literally would not let me leave, and then he would yell at me for not allowing him his peace. I still cannot believe I stayed in that situation for so long.

They rage, whether you are happy or sad. It is a way to keep you on your toes, pleasing them (abuse, pattern). Their fuel is any and all emotions. I finally realized this when I was at my worst, actually suicidal, and he laughed at me, actually told me to kill myself. When I had to get away from him, because he was actually the problem, he would kick me when I was down.

- You will never get the reaction that you want.
- You must grieve your loss anyway.
- You will never be loved back by him—not ever.
- He will lie and cheat on you, and he will lie and cheat on her.

The Break-Up(s):
So once you realize you don't want to be treated this way, you leave. I attempted to leave way before I even realized I was in an abusive relationship. It wasn't until after six failed attempts to leave and after marrying him that I finally began to understand what he was doing, what was happening to me, and that I had to get out, for good, to survive. Did you hear me? The relationship was killing me!

I would leave. Once, I drove 24 hours straight, with my dog on my lap and my daughter in the car, to my dad's in Florida. We brought only what we could fit and snuck out, after having tried to have a civil conversation with him and being threatened—I felt I had no choice. You know what he did? He took all of my belongings, twenty years of belongings—photos, irreplaceable baby videos, furniture, clothing, appliances—and he threw them out. Well, let me clarify: he had two of his employees throw them out. Months later, his dad's girlfriend told me how she had pulled a perfectly good Oreck vacuum out of the dumpster at the office. Ummm...yeah, I paid four hundred dollars for that.

WHAT ACTUALLY CONTINUED to Happen to Me?
After about two to three weeks (this never varied), he started calling. One time, he actually drove to Florida, but I wouldn't see him. Later, he flew down, and the next thing I knew, I was at the Hard Rock® with him and my daughter, celebrating New Years. It wasn't about money; it was him lying and convincing me and *me falling for it*. I fell for it many times before I actually believed his **actions over his words**. Once he had me, and he knew he had me, the act stopped. It got worse faster each time I went back. I would be crying in the mirror, trying to figure out what happened, where he was, why he was being mean, violent, abusive. I was totally confused and totally trapped, having, once again, convinced family that I was okay, that he was good.

He manipulated everyone in my life, so some of them took his side. They believed what they saw, and he showed them a lie. I had to put this, too, out of my mind to survive.

We are divorced, and he still texts my grown sons. I keep my mouth shut to keep him out of my life. My sons are smart; he won't be in their lives for long, either.

Once I realized what was happening and started to look and read and talk to other survivors I sought out through many different ways, I planned my escape—my real escape. I read, and reread in total disbelief, that they have patterns they repeat, that this was not my fault. I researched narcissism and every associated term daily until it stuck. I educated myself and reached out to resource centers, volunteering, communicating and, lastly, sharing what I learned. Others like myself saved me. Seeing I wasn't alone or at fault saved me.

THE LAW AND THE LAWYERS:

I was truly terrified for my life many times, and at least three times I called 911. The first time, he told the police I was drunk, although I had not had a single drink, of course. I was crying, and he was totally calm. I lived in his house, and we were not married. I drove a business car that he owned, and they told me to leave the residence. They said, because there was no mark on my body, it was his word against mine. He had choked me, and although my neck was red, it was not enough for the law to protect me. The second time I called 911, he had been sitting quietly at the kitchen counter, videotaping me for over an hour. When the police came, they said it was his house, and he could do whatever he wanted. This was in Spring Brook Township, PA. The last time I called 911 was when he kicked and dented my car in front of my child and chased me into my bedroom, screaming for her to leave. She was 13 and told him to go to hell—I thought he would kill both of us. We were married at that time.

The state police asked him to leave for the night and told him he should stay away. He came back at 11 p.m., turned on all the lights, and started screaming at me again. They said I should get a lawyer and that I had rights. Because there was no mark on my body, they couldn't do more but said I should get a restraining order. I went to a judge the next day, but he beat me there and got one first—it was his word against mine. I almost gave up that day. The abuser said he was being abused. I almost gave up. I simply couldn't take much more. I drove to the hospital a few times but couldn't get out of the car. I was afraid they would admit me, and I had responsibilities. The pain usually passed in about thirty minutes. I pray every day for those people who don't wait out the thirty minutes. *Please wait! This is not to say that some of us may not need longer...the pain passes is the point.* Your life is important, and you are not alone. Please, please, wait it out. Get help if needed; each one of us needs help at some point.

I was owed things, things that I lost—money, the support I gave when he opened business after business, a car, a home... something. But he had full-time attorneys, and they lied for him. Their loyalty was only to his money, and they were blind to the rest. I chose not to go that route. *I chose me; I chose life.* He threatened so many things if I fought him. I told him I didn't want to fight at all, but he would not listen. His exact words were, "If you get an attorney, you will get nothing. I would rather lose a million dollars than give you anything." I was not asking for money; I was asking for an ounce of what I lost, like help moving. I was truly afraid. I was afraid for myself, for my children, for my dogs, for my future. I knew only one thing for certain: he would not be in it. One of their biggest fears is **exposure,** but if you try to fight with a monster, you will end up hurt and he will not—no matter who wins. I am not telling you to walk away from shared property or not to fight for your children, but we did not have those things together, thank God.

The Flags I Ignored:

- His abusive and dismissive tone on the phone
- How quickly he said he loved me
- How he forced me to have sex earlier than I wanted
- **Doesn't the previous point demonstrate that I am still healing?** WOW! I should have said, "How he forced me to have sex," and that "I had sex much earlier than I wanted."
- How opinionated and prejudiced he was

- How critical he was of me and my clothes, telling me to dress sexier, to show my assets
- Telling me to wear more makeup
- Making fun of me in front of other people
- The absolute way he drove totally recklessly
- The way he made excuses about his attitudes, his verbal abuse, his rage, his driving, his behavior, his lying, his cheating
- The way he had no real friends
- The lack of connection to anyone or anything; even the home he built was for show only.
- The women's underwear I found in his bathroom
- The condoms I found in his car
- The dirty sheets I found on his bed
- The earrings I found on his bed
- The emails and photos of him with other women
- The gifts he gave to other women (the same ones he gave me at the same time)
- The way he made fun of all of his exes, saying they were all crazy or jealous
- The way he still spoke to his exes, or texted and lied to me about it
- The way he lied and cheated and called *me* jealous (lol)
- The way he tried to have sex with me in the garage, in the kitchen , in the basement, in the car—anywhere we could get caught
- The way he would grab me in public in my private parts
- The way he never took no for an answer
- The total disrespect of my boundaries
- The way he threatened me if I used an attorney during our divorce
- The way he kicked and damaged my car in front of my daughter

- The way he screamed and tried to hit me in front of my daughter
- The names he called me: ungrateful bitch, whore, and much worse
- He told me he would kill me and then himself if I went after him in any way, because I know he is a criminal and a fraud, and I have proof.

THE REALITY:

The only way to get away is to walk away and play dead. I gave no response, even as he flaunted his girlfriend he was having sex with while I was still living in his house. *She was only 22 years old.*

The only way to survive is to implement "no contact" in every possible way. If you have children or shared property or business, you still have to implement no contact. You have to protect yourself and get away, cut every string and be civil, show no emotion or reaction, ever. This is the hardest thing you will ever do, and you must do it each day, and you must do it alone. This is known as "Gray Rock."

Always be ready; they will come back. Always say no and do not engage, do not fight, do not show emotion. Once again, always **be ready, always say no and do not engage!**

WHAT HAPPENED LATER:

This crazy, amazing thing happened to me once I let myself start to heal, once I let time go by, once I grieved for my loss, for what I thought I had with him, not for him. I began to see again, see myself, my dreams, my goals…light.

Freedom and growth will come out of this if you let it. You have to let go of the anger, of the natural urge to solve the unsolvable, for closure of any kind. You will never get it. He will never love you; he never did love you. He is not sorry, and he will do it again. But you are free. He will not pay for his crimes, not without you paying double or triple. Be free, be happy—he never will. He isn't real, and he isn't good.

But you are.

XO

Moving Forward, the Eighth Year:

The worst year of my life. I finally had the courage to leave for good. His threats were screaming in my ear. He was sleeping with someone half his age. The longing for understanding and apology were finally dead. The only way to win is *not to play!* I was suicidal, and he left me there, on the floor, threatening that if I got an attorney he would kill me. **Closure** with a monster **does not exist,** and this is hard to deal with.

You have to **fight** now. Everything becomes a **trigger**! You have to hear your own voice and redirect your thoughts to be strong, retrain your brain. Realization of the subtle and constant digs and manipulation without the ability to retaliate or respond can make you feel insane. Remember: *there is no closure with these demons.* **Don't play!**

Triggers:

This is the worst part. Depression is a big surprise. Antisocial disorder, being afraid to get out of the car... A trigger could be a picture, driving in a car...you don't know until you walk away from the abuse. It could be social media or a conversation with someone.

Forget having to start your whole life over, losing all, being broke—it's the depression you will be fighting here. You need to identify the triggers and avoid them. You need to care deeply for yourself now. He will be with his new supply in the form of another woman, or fans or a new employee who is impressed by him. He will always repeat his pattern, no matter what it looks like. Pray for her.

You have to remember that what you value most is kindness, trust, and loyalty—things you can give easily but that were never given to you. In the quiet hours, I would find myself asking, *Why didn't he love me?* and that is when I knew how much work I had to do.

Going no contact is not possible right away for some of us due to the divorce process, children, or financial ties, so Gray Rock is the only option. Gray Rock is being a robot, not showing or giving up any emotions to them. Having said that, the recovery is the most brutal thing I have ever felt.

I finally allowed myself to grieve someone I hated, who assaulted me sexually, physically, but worst of all, emotionally and psychologically. I had to allow myself to be hurt and broken and go through that tunnel to begin to heal. I let go of who I wanted him to be, of who he pretended to be, but I had to grieve the love that I ACTUALLY FELT FOR HIM. This was the hardest part. Each day came with new horrors and new obvious flags that I had missed and things I wished I could have seen or changed. But I know it wasn't my fault.

I believe in order to grow, we have to own all experiences, even ones that aren't our fault. Yes, others look for goodness. Yes, they want to be us, but for me anyway, it was more. For the first time since I was 16, I was alone, without a man. I am 47 years old. I had to own that and look at it and finally change it.

I was co-dependent. I had no idea. I read a quote by psychotherapist Ross Rosenberg that said, "A better term for co-dependency is self-love deficit disorder. Lack of self-love is at the root of all co-dependent behaviors." This rang true. I realize there is no doubt now that I would never let this person back into my life. There is also, sadly, no doubt that he left a massive amount of damage in his wake in the form of my broken sense of self, my confidence, my self-worth, my self-talk. However, this is the path to CHANGE and to FREEDOM. I cannot say that I will thank him, as I am still not myself and realize I may never be, but I am free. I now just want to be with me. I hear that will change, and we will be able to find love and make better choices, but I still cannot risk it. I am too fragile; my shattered pieces have been patched back together, but the glue is not yet dry.

Everyone will look at you and think that you are okay, but you must do this work alone anyway. You must be the strongest you have ever been. For me and others who have experienced betrayal, abuse, infidelity, psychological manipulation, and financial exploitation, we were hurt beyond our capacity to understand or accept. Our very core beliefs about humanity were shaken. This is why it is so hard to get over narcissistic abuse. We need time to discover what it is to be healthy again, and we have to define that for ourselves.

From this abuse, I see my GOODNESS. I am not like you. From this EMPTINESS, I see my STRENGTH.
From the other side of this pain, I see that I am BRAVE.
From the deepness of being alone, I see my own DREAMS and remember them.
From you taking all that I gave, I see that I can
LOVE myself,
And that is HOPE…

Written by: Melissa Sachs

Almost nine months after I left for the last time, I was able to write this on my Instagram account:
And then she turned the corner, and the sun came out…

APPENDIX

Resources: Instagram contributed to my recovery in tremendous ways. Seeing how these monsters mirror one another and use the exact same playbook moves you forward in the direction of acceptance and healing. I have over 500 followers who now give me a voice to help them hear. Follow me @narccanthaveme.

There are many websites you can access. I suggest reading as much as you can. The most valuable resources come from other survivors. I used psychopathfree.com.

The magazine *Psychology Today* is also a useful tool. Articles like "Recovering from Narcissistic Abuse Without Validation" make you see that you aren't insane or the cause of any of this trauma to your life and to your brain.

You have to fight hard to move forward. You have to find strength and faith and a friend who will not judge you. Don't spend all of your time reading, because this could become a trigger. Once you understand, focus on helping others, not obsessing about narcissistic behavior. Your goal is to get away from it and learn from it and heal and help others.

www.ingramcontent.com/pod-product-compliance
Lightning Source LLC
Chambersburg PA
CBHW070628300426
44113CB00010B/1702